Prophecy & the Last Pope

Saint Malachy, Nostradamus, the Antichrist, and End Times

by
Dace Allen and Sarah Skye

DISCLAIMER

This information in book is provided as entertainment. Information is based on personal experience and anecdotal reports, and should not replace legal, medical, religious or other professional advice. Readers assume full responsibility for use of the information in this book.

The authors do not speak for the Catholic Church, and the church has not endorsed anything in this book.

To contact the authors by mail, please write to
Sarah Skye c/o New Forest Books
PO Box 2216
Concord, NH 03302-2216 USA

To reach the authors by email, write to email@SarahSkye.com

Library of Congress Cataloging-in-Publication Data
Allen, Dace (1951 -) and Skye, Sarah (1969 -)
Prophecy & the Last Pope / Dace Allen and Sarah Skye. -- 1st ed.
ISBN 978-1482568929   (pbk.)
1. Religion--prophecy. 2. Religion--Christianity--Catholic.
I. Title

Edited by Margaret Brighton.
Cover design by Amy Hewitt. Cover illustrations (L to R) by xiquinhosilva, Sergey Gabdurakhmanov, Sergey Kozhukhov under a Creative Commons, Share-Alike license. If you'd like a free copy of the cover for your own use (under that license), contact the authors.

NEW FOREST
BOOKS

Production coordinated by New Forest Books.

Table of Contents

Introduction

"With full freedom I declare that I renounce the ministry of Bishop of Rome, Successor of Saint Peter, entrusted to me by the Cardinals on 19 April 2005, in such a way, that as from 28 February 2013, at 20:00 hours, the See of Rome, the See of Saint Peter, will be vacant..."

With those words on February 11th, 2013, Pope Benedict XVI astonished the world. Christians and non-Christians reeled with amazement. Even the Pope's spokesman, Federico Lombardi, said the news "took us by surprise."

Less than a week before, the Pope's tweets had been very mild. He'd said, "Everything is a gift from God: it is only by recognizing this crucial dependence on the Creator that we will find freedom and peace."

For most people, there were no *obvious* clues that the Pope was about to resign.

In fact, Benedict XVI may have been looking ahead to this eventuality for several *years*. In a 2010 interview, Benedict explained that when the Pope "is no longer physically, psychologically and spiritually capable of handling the duties of his office, then he has a right and, under some circumstances, also an obligation to resign."

In April 2012, *Der Spiegel* mentioned a decline in the Pope's health. "The mood at the Vatican is apocalyptic. Pope Benedict XVI seems tired, and both unable and unwilling to seize the reins amid fierce infighting and scandal."

At the time, that seemed a little harsh. Now we know that the Pope was *very* aware of the issues. He was already making plans for his future.

As soon as Pope Benedict XVI announced his resignation, rumors began to circulate. Some were wilder than others. Claims of impending Alzheimer's or dementia rivaled the insistence that documents implicated the pope in a *vast* cover-up of misconduct by priests. News stories claimed that Benedict was seeking asylum from the Italian government. Those stories suggested impending charges and even *more* sexual improprieties by Catholic clergy.

Other stories described attempts to kill Pope Benedict. One story slipped out early in 2012, after an Italian cardinal's visit to China. The official response..? Vatican spokesman Federico Lombardi said the report was "so completely beyond reality and hardly serious that I don't even want to consider it."

Remembering Watergate, we'd call that a "non-denial denial."

Others noticed a steady stream of news reports about the Pope's health. The pacemaker issue. The 2012 head injury. And so on.

Were those smokescreens, or pre-emptive media efforts, to raise sympathy for the ailing Pope? Will reports like those prevent him for being judged too harshly if (or perhaps when) more tales of money-laundering, corruption, and other scandals emerge?

The truth may be simple: The Pope's health has been deteriorating. He was not a young man when he accepted the Papacy nearly eight years ago. In fact, *he was the oldest cardinal elected Pope in nearly 300 years.*

Comments by the Pope's brother, Georg, confirmed that Pope Benedict XVI's activities were increasingly limited by his doctor's admonitions. That's normal for any 85-year-old man. With Pope Benedict XVI's schedule and responsibilities, it's no wonder his doctor was concerned.

Or, if all of this drama was planned — as early as the 1960s, according to some — perhaps Benedict outlived his expected time, *and he knows it.* The strength of the word "renounce" suggests that he's distancing himself from the Papacy. We suspect he chose his words carefully.

Most people have forgotten Benedict's 2005 uneasy comments when he was elected Pope:

"As the trend in the ballots slowly made me realize that — in a manner of speaking the guillotine would fall on me — I started to feel quite dizzy.

"I thought that I had done my life's work and could now hope to live out my days in peace.

"I told the Lord with deep conviction, 'Don't do this to me. You have younger and better (candidates) who could take up this great task with a totally different energy and with different strength.'"

What's next for the Papacy and the Catholic Church? Is the arrival of *Petrus Romanus* — perhaps the Antichrist — imminent? Is he already here? How will we recognize him?

People are turning to prophecies like those of Saint Malachy.

- St. Malachy listed just 111 Popes in his 12th century predictions. Benedict XVI was #111. Pope Francis, the 112th leader of the Catholic Church may *not* be what the faithful expect.
- Reports say that St. Paul's Church in Roman has room for only *one* more Papal portrait after Benedict XVI's.
- The crypt at St. Peter's Basilica has space for just *two* people: Benedict XVI and Pope Francis. Is that the end of the line?

Other tales and prophecies raise more hopeful expectations, but we can't ignore the darker ones.

In this book, we hope to answer the most popular questions about St. Malachy's *Prophecy of the Popes,* the "last Pope" theories, *Petrus Romanus* (Peter of Rome), and how they relate to the Antichrist and the end of the world.

We've researched among ancient news reports and archaic documents, in dusty libraries and "hiding in plain sight" resources. What we found may surprise you.

Dace Allen and Sarah Skye

1. Which Prophecies Describe the Last Pope?

In this book, we'll use the word "prophet" to describe *someone who makes prophecies.* That's different from a *prophet of God.*

The Catholic church has not approved or verified most end-time prophecies in this book.

However, many prophecies talk about the last Pope. Many of them echo each other. In some cases, that's deliberate. In others, it's eerie enough to make us start humming *Twilight Zone* music.

Despite our sometimes-flippant attitudes, we *do* take these claims seriously. We just prefer not to get all doom-and-gloom about the topic. In almost every credible end-time prophecy, we find a silver lining if we look for it. It may be five pages before or after the actual prediction, but it's usually there.

So, don't think we're being irreverent. We wouldn't have put long hours into this research if we thought it was a joke. And, in case you have any doubt, we each read our Scriptures at the start of every day. We *are* religious people.

So, let's talk about prophecies...

For many centuries, prophets have talked about the Popes, especially the man who will be the very *last* Pope. Prophets have also described the end of the world, the return of Christ, and the beginning of the Millennium. They're momentous events. We understand people's concerns. At some point, *everyone* wonders about *some* of these issues. However, only a few make important predictions.

When some prophecies — like those attributed to St. Malachy — come true, people take notice. Those are the kinds of prophecies we — especially Dace — have been studying for *years*. They're fascinating.

However, it's a mistake to think that — just because a prophet got *one* prediction exactly right (or was even close to accurate) — *all* of his or her predictions are equally accurate. As the saying goes, "Even a *broken* watch gives the correct time twice a day." (In Saint Malachy's case, he's been wrong — or seemed to completely miss the mark — just four times out of over 100. Those are pretty convincing odds in his favor.)

But, we had to draw the line somewhere when we were writing this book. Some prophecies are better than others. Many that we read... they were great, and might fit a later book, but not this one.

We aimed for a cross-section of credible predictions related to the Pope, and — when the prophecies talk about things like comets — events that might signal the arrival of the "last Pope."

12th century – St. Malachy's *Prophecy of the Popes*

The most famous prophecies about the last Pope were attributed to Saint Malachy of Ireland (1094 – 1148). His list of 111 Popes (or possibly 112) wasn't revealed until the 16th century.

In one version of the story, the prophecies were documented by St. Bernard, in whose arms St. Malachy died. Bernard sent the prophecies to the Pope. Realizing the importance of those prophecies, the Pope placed them in storage near the Vatican, for safekeeping and to be revealed at the appropriate time.

In the late 1500s, Benedictine historian Arnold de Wyon (or Wion) found those papers and published the prophecies as part of a massive tome, *Lignum Vitæ*. (Lignum vitae is Latin for "ironwood," one of the hardest and most long-lasting of commercial woods, and — in the era of Wyon — believed to have medicinal properties.) The prophecies were in a section of the book called *Prophetia S. Malachiae, Archiepiscopi, of Summis Pontificibus.* (Translated, that means something like: Prophecy of St.

Malachy, Archbishop, of the Last or Supreme Popes.)

In another version of the story, the document was created in the late 16th century. It was merely *attributed* to St. Malachy to avoid questioning and persecution during the years of Inquisition. (Generally, from late 1100s through the mid-1800s.)

We'll talk about Saint Malachy's predictions — and the many issues related to their origins — later in this book.

Currently, many people are interested in the 111th Pope predicted by Saint Malachy, perhaps the last *real* Pope. That was Benedict XVI. He surprised the world with his resignation, early in 2013.

St. Malachy described Pope Benedict XVI as "Gloria Olivae," or "the glory of the olive." That's all St. Malachy said about him. That phrase describes Pope Benedict XVI in many unique ways.

- Cardinal Joseph Ratzinger chose his papal name, Pope Benedict XVI, after Pope Benedict XV (Pope during World War I) and St. Benedict of Nursia, the founder of the Benedictine Order.

- The crest of the Benedictine order contains an olive branch.

- Saint Benedict predicted that, *shortly before the end of the world,* the Olivetans would lead the Catholic Church. "Olivetans" is a term that can mean the Benedictine Order. If you broaden that to include *all* followers of Saint Benedict, Pope Benedict XVI has been an Olivetan.

- In addition, as Cardinal Ratzinger, Benedict XVI had been Cardinal-Bishop of Velletri-Segni. The coat of arms of Velletri includes three olive trees. The crest of the Italian Republic also contains an olive branch. So, Benedict XVI had an *abundance* of "olive" connections, and *far* more than most people.

Now, we get to the *interesting* part of the final prophecies of Saint Malachy: *Petrus Romanus.*

Petrus Romanus

After the Pope designated Gloria Olivae, St. Malachy reportedly predicted the final leader of the church as *Petrus Romanus*. That's usually translated as "Peter the Roman," or "Peter of Italy."

St. Malachy said:

> Petrus Romanus, qui paſcet oues in multis tribulationibus: quibus tranſactis ciuitas ſepticollis diruetur, & Iudex tremdus iudicabit populum ſuum.

Here's one translation:

> "In the final persecution of the Holy Roman Church there will reign *Petrus Romanus,* who will feed his flock amid many tribulations, after which the seven-hilled city will be destroyed and the dreadful Judge will judge the people. The End."

Some have interpreted this (possible) 112th Pope in the sequence as the antichrist or Satan.

A few have further insisted that he'd have a dark countenance. (That expression can mean many things, including — but not necessarily — dark skin.)

> Before the conclave, the leading candidates for Pope included Cardinal Peter Turkson of Ghana, Cardinal Marc Ouelet of Canada, and Cardinal Francis Arinze of Nigeria. If the next Pope had been *Peter* Turkson or Odilo *Pedro* Scherer, that would have matched the Malachy prophecy, *exactly.*

Whether the "dark" or "black" reference in many "last Pope" prophecies (not necessarily St. Malachy's) is true, we're not certain.

- Pope Francis *is* a Jesuit, and he's been known for favoring the simple, black cassock of that order.

Is Pope Francis *Petrus Romanus?* He fits that description in several ways. Is this a signal that the end of the world is approaching?

Not necessarily.

Maybe it was a coincidence when Pope Francis used the phrase "end of the world" in his March 13th speech (2013)?

- The Pope said, "Sembra che i miei fratelli cardinali sono andati a prenderlo quasi alla **fine del mondo**." (emphasis added) It was quickly translated as, "It seems the cardinals have gone to the end of the earth to pick me." That may be true. However, the "fine del mondo" phrase put many people on high alert. They claim it's a "hiding in plain sight" clue to the drama about to unfold.

Don't panic. There may be a few more Popes *before* Petrus Romanus... but we're getting ahead of ourselves. (In the *next* chapter, we'll talk about the possibility of a break in the timeline.)

Let's cruise through some *other* prophecies that tell us about the last Pope and the end of the world as we know it.

12th century – Saint Hildegard

Hildegard of Bingen (1098 – 1179), also known as Saint Hildegard or Sibyl of the Rhine, was noted for her many extraordinary gifts, including healing and prophecy. She was *also* a member of the Order of Saint Benedict.

Her predictions included a time when people would reject the Pope and prefer their own church leaders. (She was very independent-minded, but still... in her lifetime, rejecting the Pope was almost unthinkable.)

She also predicted:

> "**Before the comet comes**, many nations, *the good excepted,* will be scourged by want and famine. The great nation in the ocean that is inhabited by people of different tribes and descent will be devastated by earthquake, storm, and tidal wave. It will be divided and, in great part,

submerged. That nation will also have many misfortunes at sea and lose its colonies. After the great Comet, the great nation will be devastated by earthquakes, storms, and great waves of water, causing much want and plagues. The ocean will also flood many other countries, so that all coastal cities will live in fear, with many destroyed. **All sea coast cities will be fearful,** and many of them will be destroyed by tidal waves, and most living creatures will be killed, and even those who escape will die from a horrible disease. **For in none of those cities does a person live according to the Laws of God.** A powerful wind will rise in the North, carrying heavy fog and the densest dust, and it will fill their throats and eyes so that they will cease their butchery and be stricken with a great fear."

Does this relate to the Vatican? Rome — including the Vatican — is about nine miles from the seacoast. We're not sure if that qualifies as a "sea coast city."

The "comet" may be Comet ISON — expected to reach Earth's orbit on November 1st and, due to its proximity to the sun, achieve peak visibility around November 28th, 2013 — which is supposed to be the brightest comet ever seen.

But, it might be something else. The meteorite that struck Russia's Ural Mountains on 15 February 2013... that *could* look like a comet to a visionary. So, we're not pinning Hildegard's prediction to ISON, but we don't think the February 2013 meteorite could be called a "great comet," no matter *how* startling the vision might seem at the time.

However, when we talk about "silver linings" in our research, we note that Hildegard referenced terrible times in certain cities... but "in none of those cities does a person live according to the Laws of God." So, we're optimistic that things won't be so dire for people in communities that *do* include God-fearing people who live accordingly.

Keep in mind, Hildegard's prophecies were wide-reaching.

For example, she spoke of a divided Germany in the future. In an era when women were still considered property, and described as creatures who must be protected from their own sinful natures, it's notable that her prophecies were taken so seriously by her contemporaries.

13th century – Abbot Werdin

Abbot Werdin of Otranto, also known as Abbot Werdin d'Orante or d'Otrante, died in 1279.

He said:

> **"The great monarch and the great Pope will precede the Antichrist.** The nations will be at war for four years and a great part of the world will be destroyed. The Pope will go over the sea carrying the sign of Redemption on his forehead. The great Monarch will come to restore peace and the Pope will share in the victory."

In many of these predictions, the combination of a great monarch and a great Pope are mentioned. It's kind of a running theme in some of these prophecies. We're pretty sure they're two different people, but we wonder... In the future, might there be *shared* leadership of the Catholic Church?

13th century – Caesarius of Heisterbach

Caesarius of Heisterbach was a Cistercian monk who lived in Cologne from 1180 to 1240.

He's best remembered for quoting Arnaud Amalric. Amalric, asked about separating Catholics from Cathars during the Albigensian Crusade (1209 – 1229), replied, *"Caedite eos. Novit enim Dominus qui sunt eius,"* or "Slay them. God knows his own." This statement is often remembered as "Kill them all and let God sort them out." (The failure of the Albigensian Crusade led directly to the Medieval Inquisition.)

In general, Caesarius sounds like a quirky guy, if a bit pessimistic. He was also a prophet, and predicted that, at a future time:

> "**There will be no Pope,** and the air will be as a pestilence, destroying men and beasts alike. Not since the creation of the world has one experienced such misfortune."

13th century – Johannes Friede

Johannes Friede (1204 – 1257) was an Austrian monk and a member of the Order of St. John. His prophecies ranged from murky to very precise. Some of his precise predictions are the most difficult to understand. They describe calamities, but nothing clearly related to the Pope.

> "**When the great time will come, in which mankind will face its last, hard trial**, it will be foreshadowed by **striking changes in nature**; the alteration between cold and heat will become more intensive, storms will have more catastrophic effects, earthquakes will destroy greater regions and the seas will overflow many lowlands. Not all of it will be the result of natural causes, but man will penetrate into the bowels of the earth and will reach into the clouds, gambling with its own existence. Before the powers of destruction will succeed in their design, the universe will be thrown into disorder, and the age of iron will plunge into nothingness. When the nights will be filled with more intensive cold and the day with heat, a new life will begin in nature. The heat means radiation from the earth, the cold the waning light of the sun. Only a few more years and you will become aware that sunlight has become perceptibly weaker. When even your artificial light will cease to give service, the great event of the firmament will be near."

He then talks about the "nebula of the Greater Bear" — Ursa Major, also known as the Big Dipper — approaching Earth, and light coming from Orion, not the moon. (Also see Job 9:9; 38:32.)

> "Finally, complete darkness will set in and last for three days and three nights... During this time,

men, deprived of the power of light, will fall into a slumber-like sleep from which many will not awaken, especially those who have no spark of spiritual life. When the sun will again rise and emerge, earth will be covered with a blanket of ashes like snow in winter, except that the ashes will have the color of sulfur. Damp fog will ascend from the ground, illuminated by igneous gases.

"...On the seventh day after the return of light, earth will have absorbed the ashes and formed such a fertility as has not been experienced ever before. But Orion will cast its ray on the earth and show a path toward the last resting place of the greatest and most eminent man who had ever lived on the earth. The survivors will proclaim his ancient doctrine in peace and will institute the millennium, **announced by the Messiah** in the light of true brotherly and sisterly love for the glory of the Creator and for the blessedness of all mankind."

It's rather cryptic and references the Millennium, but nothing clearly related to the Pope.

- The first passage, above, *might* suggest climate change.
- The darkness and sulphuric ash *might* indicate something like an explosion of the Yellowstone Caldera (USA).
- The proximity of Ursa Major *might* mean a polar shift.

Or, they might mean something else altogether.

The environmental references in those predictions are *so* startling and interesting, we decided to include them.

16th century – Nostradamus

Nostradamus, one of the great visionaries and prophets of all time, needs no introduction. Here's one of his quatrains that may be relevant:

Century 2, Quatrain 41

> The great star will burn for seven days,
> The cloud will cause two suns to appear:
> The big mastiff will howl all night
> When the great pontiff will change country.

In many prophecies, we've seen references to the Pope fleeing from the Vatican, and perhaps from Rome and Italy, altogether. So, keep this quatrain in mind. The "two suns" could be the daytime sighting of the *great comet* referenced in other predictions.

We'll talk about Nostradamus' other relevant predictions, later in this book.

16th century - Jean de Vitiguerro

So far, aside from oft-repeated prediction, below, the history of this individual is confusing. Bear with us as we try to explain.

We've found references to Vitiguerro *translating* the following from the Latin to French in 1831. Other records mention his literary works in 1814.

Then, author Thomas A. Kselman, in his 1983 book, *Miracles and Prophecies in 19th Century France,* describes Jean de Vitiguerro as the author of *Mirablis Libre,* published in 1524. The book was a compilation of Medieval predictions.

That means Vitiguerro wasn't doing the *translating* in the early 1800s; he was an earlier *author* whose *works* were being translated — probably by Edouard Bricon in France — in the 19th century.

So, if you stumble onto prophecies attributed to Vitiguerro, make sure the reporter knows what he or she is talking about. Too many authors copy references from each other. Always try to go back to primary sources if you can, and secondary sources as needed. By the time something is being reported by someone six degrees from the original materials, it can lose a lot in the translation. Sometimes, literally.

Apparently, Vitiguerro was also known as Jean

Prêcheguerre, Jean Vatigero or Vatigera, John of Vatiguerro and Joannes of Vatiguerro. (Remember, in some countries, names weren't standardized until the 19th century or so. Ditto the standardization of spelling.)

Kselman suggests that Vitiguerro was one of the most prominent of prophets admired during the period known as the Restoration. Generally, people believe that he lived in the 16th century — not the 13th, as widely attributed — and *his work influenced Nostradamus*. Really.

Regardless of the author's history, the prophecy is *very* specific:

> "**The pope will change his residence** and the Church will not be defended for **twenty-five months or more** because, during all that time **there will be no Pope in Rome**... After many tribulations, a Pope shall be elected out of those who survived the persecutions."

Some people are pointing to the move of Pope Benedict XVI to his summer residence, and then to a monastery. We guess they thought it might take nearly *two years* for the Catholic Church to appoint a new Pope...?

But, what if Pope Francis is — for some reason — not a *real* Pope? We're not sure how that might be, but as we sort through prophecy and speculation, we need to consider *every* possibility.

We're also not sure how that fits with St. Malachy's unusual reference to *Peter the Roman*, which is so different from how Malachy indicated the other Popes.

One small note: John of Vitiguerro has also been erroneously attributed with the "Before the comet..." prediction of St. Hildegard. Watch out for that when you're doing your own research. If you see that kind of mistake, there may be other mistakes in the work, as well.

However, Vitiguerro — or at least his book — was also attributed with the following predictions, very loosely translated from the French:

"We will see in the sky of many signs and surprising, the sun will appear obscure and the color of blood in the eyes of many people. We'll see once, for about four hours, **two moons at the same time**, they will appear with several amazing things and worthy of admiration. A star will signal the destruction and massacre of almost all men.

"... **But after the whole universe has been plagued by hardships and miseries...by the will of God a Pope will be elected.** He will have escaped the persecution of the Church. He will be a very holy man, endowed with all perfection and will be crowned by saints and angels. He will be placed on the Holy See by his brothers who, exiled with him, survived **the persecutions of the Church.**

"This Pope will reform the entire universe by his holiness and bring it to the old way of life... He will preach barefoot and not fear the power of princes.

"**The Pope will have with him an emperor,** very virtuous man, who will carry in him the holy blood of the kings of France. The prince will be in aid and obey him in everything to reform the universe. And under this Pope and the emperor, the world will be reformed, and God's wrath will subside... peace will last for many years."

So, in that prophecy, we see the idea of two moons. Might that be a comet and a moon?

Then, there's a time when there is no Pope, or at least no Pope in Rome. (Is it that *fleeing from Rome* theme that we keep seeing? We're not sure.)

Finally, there's another reference to a Pope plus a monarch, in this case: an emperor.

We like that this prophecy has a happy ending, with peace lasting for many years. It sounds like we'll be ready for it.

16th century – Mother Shipton

Mother Shipton is a legend, and someone we know little

about. According to stories, she was born Ursula Southeil in England around 1488, and was known throughout England for the accuracy of her predictions. Poems she wrote talk about the future. Whether they refer to the Pope or not, remains to be seen. Often, her predictions are best understood — and remarkably clear, in context — *after* they occur.

Part of one of her poems includes this dire vision of the future:

> The kings shall false promise make
> And talk just for talking's sake
> And nations plan horrific war
> The like as never seen before
> And taxes rise and lively down
> And nations wear perpetual frown.
>
> Yet greater sign there be to see
> As man nears latter century
> Three sleeping mountains gather breath
> And spew out mud, and ice and death.
> And earthquakes swallow town and town,
> In lands as yet to me unknown.
>
> **And christian one fights christian two**
> And nations sigh, yet nothing do
> And yellow men great power gain
> From mighty bear with whom they've lain.
>
> These mighty tyrants will fail to do
> They fail to split the world in two.
> But from their acts a danger bred
> An ague – leaving many dead.
> And physics find no remedy
> For this is worse than leprosy.
>
> Oh many signs for all to see
> The truth of this true prophecy.

See the Appendix in this book for more of her predictions. You can tell that she's having fun, being a little cryptic while — at the same time — speaking plainly. In our opinion, she must have been a very bright woman.

Some of her poems have been questioned because they were published so long after her death, and because we know at least one person — Charles Hindley, in 1862 — altered her poems before publishing them.

Also, none *clearly* indicate anything *papal* — except lines like "christian one fights christian two" and (from another poem, which some say references Comet ISON) "A fiery dragon will cross the sky / Six times before this earth shall die... For seven days and seven nights / Man will watch this awesome sight... And when the dragon's tail is gone, Man forgets, and smiles, and carries on / To apply himself – too late, too late / For mankind has earned deserved fate./ His masked smile – his false grandeur, Will serve the Gods their anger stir."

Then there are lines that, to us, sound like some alliance in Asia. Could the "bear" be Russia or the former U.S.S.R.? The U.S.S.R. had been North Korea's staunchest supporter, and actually supplied the tanks used by North Korea to launch the Korean War. North Korea could be the "yellow men," and in menacing rhetoric about South Korea, North Korea has described itself as a "tiger."

Mother Shipton's poems are fascinating. Nevertheless, because of their uncertain authenticity, we advise against taking these predictions very seriously.

17th century – Venerable Bartholomew Holzhauser

Bartholomew Holzhauser (1613 – 1658) was a German priest and the founder of the Bartholomewites, also known as the United Order, sometimes called Communists, later called the Apostolic Order of Secular Priests.

He was a visionary and predicted:

> "The fifth period of the Church, which began circa 1520, will end with the arrival of **the holy Pope and of the powerful Monarch** who is called "Help From God" because he will restore everything. The fifth period is one of affliction, desolation, humiliation, and poverty for the

Church... These are the evil times, a century full of dangers and calamities. Heresy is everywhere, and the followers of heresy are in power almost everywhere. **but God will permit a great evil against His Church:** Heretics and tyrants will come suddenly and unexpectedly; they will break into the Church. They will enter Italy and lay Rome waste; they will burn down churches and destroy everything."

Okay. It's not cheerful stuff. However, some of these themes keep repeating, and we don't think these people were going out of their way to copy each other. So, we're still watching for the Pope + monarch combination.

18th century – Jeanne le Royer

Jeanne le Royer (1731 – 1798) of Boulot, Fougeres, Brittany, was a nun among the Sisters of the Nativity. She became famous after predicting the French Revolution. The following predictions are loosely translated from the French.

About the church, she predicted:

"I see that when the Second Coming of Christ approaches **a bad priest will do much harm to the Church**..."

Speaking about heresy entering the church in the latter days, she said:

"It will be like a fire burning underneath, quietly, and be spread gradually. This is even more serious and dangerous, for the Holy Church will not notice these early fires."

"O God! I see the agitation of the Holy Church, when she will realize, suddenly, the increasing size and number of ungodly souls they have drawn into their party! This heresy extends so far that it appears to include all countries. Never any heresy has been so deadly!"

She also said that Jesus told her:

> "... the first two decades of the century in 2000 will
> not pass without judgment..."

To us, her "fires" might be the misconduct of priests, too long overlooked. It's cost the Catholic Church dearly, and we're not just talking in dollars and cents.

And, from the viewpoint of the first decades of the 21st century, the Church has *not* escaped some harsh judgment.

18th century – Helena Walraff

> "The Pope will be forced to flee, followed by four
> cardinals. [Alternate translation: "accompanied by
> only four cardinals.] He will find refuge in Koeln
> (Cologne)."

Once again, we're seeing a prediction about the Pope fleeing. This one is precise, about four cardinals following or accompanying him. (We'd leave that open. After all, the four cardinals might be *chasing* him, or they might be fleeing *with* him.)

However, while many of these kinds of prophecies mention the Pope finding safety (at least temporarily) in France, this prediction talks about Cologne, Germany's fourth-largest city. Perhaps the Pope rests in Cologne for some time, and then has to flee further west, to France?

19th century – Anna Katherine Emmerich

Anna Katherine Emmerich (1774 – 1824) was a German nun of the Augustine convent. She was also a visionary and stigmatic. An intense investigation of her stigmata proved them to be genuine.

Her predictions included an assertion that the Papacy will be replaced by a council of twelve apostolic disciples. Together with the people, they will bring forth a renewal of spiritual life. She also said, "...The Jews shall return to Palestine, and become Christians toward the end of the world."

Others' prophecies have talked about a time of "no Pope." So, we're wondering if there might be a change. Maybe the church *will* choose a leadership of twelve disciples. (We've noticed that Emmerich didn't specify men or women disciples, just the general term, "disciples.")

The Jews moving into Palestine sounds *odd,* but not as strange as Jews becoming Christians. Not when they're so close to Israel, anyway. That's a future we have difficulty picturing.

Modern prophecy

20th century – Father R. Gerald Culleton

Father Culleton is considered one of the most complete authorities on the subject of the Antichrist. He's the author of books including *The Reign of Antichrist* and *Prophets in Our Times.*

Father Culleton has predicted:

> "A schism of short duration is destined to break out...An antipope, of German origin, is to be set up, and finally **Rome itself will be destroyed**."

Cardinal Ratzinger — Pope Benedict XVI — had German ancestry. And, to the surprise of many, he's retaining his rank as Pope and will continue to wear the white cassock, even after retiring. In the truest sense of past "antipope" designations, he *could* be described with that term.

20th century – Edgar Cayce

Edgar Cayce — dubbed "the sleeping prophet" because he would receive his visions while in an apparent slumber, trance, or deep meditation — predicted that there would be just *one* real Pope after John Paul II. We doubt that he'd read Saint Malachy's prophecies, so his prediction is especially interesting.

21st century – Ellie Crystal

Ms. Crystal has a lot to say about mystical and prophetic issues related to the Pope. Some are more credible than others, but one cannot dispute the surprising accuracy of some of her predictions.

One (coincidence?) that we found most interesting was when Ms. Crystal pointed out that Pope Benedict XVI was the 256th Pope, and his numeric designation as Benedict (16), squared, was also 256.

We talk more about numerology in a later chapter. Coincidences like this, while not *prophetic,* are interesting.

2. What Was St. Malachy's Prophecy?

Saint Malachy (1094 - 1148) was an Irish priest, reportedly from the city of Dublin.

Later in his career, he was best known as the Archbishop of Armagh (Ireland), and a visionary. Around 1139, during a journey to Rome to meet Pope Innocent II, Malachy fell into a deep trance. That's generally attributed to a witnessed event on Janiculum Hill, referred to as "the eighth hill of Rome."

In a vision, Malachy saw a long line of Popes from 1134 -- after the death of Pope Innocent II -- to what seems like the end of the world. In some versions of the story, a companion with Malachy took out writing tools and transcribed what Saint Malachy uttered.

That list -- of 111 or 112 Popes -- has been called the *Prophecy of the Popes.* Then-bishop Malachy presented the list to Innocent II, who recognized the importance of the document. Innocent II had it placed in the Vatican archives for safekeeping. However, there was no Vatican library at that time. Records were stored here and there, around Rome, in basements and closets. It was a haphazard system, in contrast with the Vatican repositories of more modern times.

Nevertheless, the Malachy document was rediscovered by Benedictine monk and historian Arnold de Wyon of Monte Cassino, and it was published in 1595. (We'll talk more about Arnold de Wyon and Monte Cassino in a later chapter. Trust us, it's an interesting part of the story.)

Similar to Nostradamus' quatrains, Malachy had indicated each Pope with a motto or short verse in Latin. The theory is: Those vague references left the votes in the hands of the cardinals, and did not impinge on their free will to elect the man *they* chose based solely on merits and inspiration.

And, the fact is, some of those references were truly obscure. Sure, there's Innocent XIII, "of a good religion." That could be any Pope. Ditto Pius VIII, "religious man."

But, even with perfect hindsight, how did anyone come up with "snaky man" for Gregory X? His family's coat of arms showed a large serpent devouring a male child, feet first. That's pretty obscure, and -- to us -- it supports the idea that a visionary like Saint Malachy *was* behind the prophecies.

Malachy's predictions were uncanny. His accuracy still astonishes people.

For example, here are some descriptions from recent church history:

104. Religio depopulata (Religion laid waste, or religion depopulated)

This was Pope Benedict XV (in office between 1914 and1922). Communism moved into Russia, the very religious Czar of Russia and his family were murdered, and countless Christians died during World War I.

105. Fides intrepida (Faith fearless)

Pope Pius XI (1922 - 1939) spoke out against Communism and Fascism, even though Italy had become a fascist state. Though the Pope was under considerable pressure, within and outside the church, he remained firm in his faith. Following his own motto of "Christ's peace in Christ's kingdom," Pope Pius XI successfully defended and protected the church from attacks by the Italian government, and ended those hostilities with the Lateran Treaty of 1929. Some believe that his sudden death (from a heart attack) may have been murder, since his primary doctor was the father of Mussolini's mistress. Possible...? Yes. Likely...? We're not so sure.

106. Pastor angelicus (Angelic pastor)

Pope Pius XII (1939 - 1958) was a visionary. The day that he was consecrated as bishop was the same day that the Virgin Mary first appeared at Fatima. Pius XII balanced a renewal of sacred traditions, including the restoration of Easter Vigils, while increasing the number of non-Latin services and decentralizing the church's authority. According to some, Pius received numerous spiritual visions throughout his life. Though described as "hallucinations" by some of Pius' detractors, the truth cannot be determined until details of those visions are finally made public.

107. Pastor & Nauta (Pastor and mariner)

Pope John XXIII (1958 - 1963), prior to being elected Pope, was the Patriarch of Venice. The "mariner" connection is obvious.

108. Flos Florum (Flower of flowers)

Pope Paul VI (1963 - 1978) used a coat of arms that included three fleurs-de-lis, or iris blossoms.

109. De medietate Luna (At the middle of the Moon, or half of the moon)

The reign of Pope John Paul I (1978) lasted just 33 days, starting at the middle of the Moon's cycle and ending at the middle of the next cycle. The mid-point of his reign was September 17th, the date of a lunar eclipse. For someone to just *guess* this -- in 1595 or earlier -- is impressive. To us, it indicates a credible prophet.

110. De Labore Solus (The labor of the sun, or an eclipse)

Pope John Paul II (1978 - 2005) was born on 18 May 1920, when the sun was at near total eclipse. He was entombed on 5 April 2005, also the day of a solar eclipse. (What *most* interested us was a 1797 book in which author Sylvanus Urban specifically translates this Papal reference in terms of a solar eclipse... two centuries before it happened. That removes the likelihood that Malachy's Latin phrases were re-translated in a revisionist style. Given *multiple* ways to interpret the Sun reference, who goes with something as rare as an eclipse? Only a true prophet with an unshakeable vision of future events.)

111. Gloria Olivae (The glory of the olive)

Pope Benedict XVI (2005 - 2013) chose his name out of respect for Pope Benedict XV, who was Pope during WW I, and in memory of St. Benedict of Nursia, the founder of the

Benedictine monasteries. The Benedictine order's symbols include an olive branch. And, Jesus delivered his most apocalyptic speech -- the Olivet discourse or Olivet prophecy (Mark 13, Matthew 24, Luke 21) -- from the Mount of Olives.

The punctuation issue

At that point in the Malachy prophecies, the predictions aren't as clear. One problem is the break in the lines (seen in the scan of Wyon's 1595 book, below). There is a period after *sedebit,* possibly indicating the end of the verse.

If the last section is actually *two* sections, not one run-on sentence, there might be additional Popes *between* Benedict XVI and the leadership of Peter of Rome.

First, the partial line in question: *In persecutione extrema S.R.E. sedebit.* Translated, that means, "in extreme persecution, the Holy Roman Church (Sancta Romana Ecclesia) will sit."

If that's where the verse breaks, we don't know how long the Holy Roman Church will "sit."

After that, *Petrus Romanus, qui paſcet oues in multis tribulationibus: quibus tranſactis ciuitas ſepticollis diruetur, & Iudex tremedus iudicabit populum ſuum. Finis.*

Translated, that's "Peter the Roman (or Peter of Rome), who will feed his sheep in many tribulations, which being accomplished, the seven-hilled city (Rome) shall be utterly destroyed, and the dreadful Judge shall call the people to judgment. The End."

However, if the entire passage is *one* sentence, it's usually translated: "In the last persecution, Peter, a Roman, shall possess the seat of the Holy Roman Church, and feed the sheep in many tribulations; which being accomplished, the city of seven hills shall fall and the dreadful Judge shall call the people to judgment. The End."

In the latter version, it's often interpreted that *Peter the Roman* is the Antichrist.

Those are two *very* different predictions, and *we don't know which one is correct.* Unfortunately, Arnold de Wyon was fairly liberal with his use of periods.

(Since the two-sentence version is supported by numerical analysis, we lean *slightly* towards the former, in which the church sits... and *then* Peter the Roman arrives, at a later time. See our chapter, "Nostradamus, Numerology, and the Last Pope," for the numbers. However, as a writing team, we're divided -- polarized, really -- on how seriously to weigh the numerological evidence. It's *interesting,* but not all of us are certain it's *compelling* evidence.

However, if the story *is* true about St. Paul's Church having space in the Papal gallery for only *one* more portrait after Benedict XVI's, and -- as of the imminent retirement of Benedict XVI -- only *two* more empty spaces in the crypt at St. Peter's Basilica, it seems as if there will be just one more Pope. It might be Peter the Roman, or it might be one Pope between Benedict XVI and Peter the Roman.

After all, in the latter translation, the prediction only says that *Peter will occupy the seat of the Holy Roman Church.* It doesn't say he'll be *Pope.*

Either way, it's unlikely that anyone will be *Pope Peter.* Since the beginning of the church, there's been an unspoken rule that no Pope will take the name of Peter.

On the next page, you'll see part of the original page, reportedly from the original 1595 book.

The lower, far right column includes the debated passage about Peter the Roman (Petrus Romanus).

Liber Secundus. 311.

co , Cardinalis creatus à Pio. IIII, qui pi-
la in armis geſtabat.

Axis in medietate ſigni.Sixtus. V. qui axem in medio Leonis in ar-
　　　　　mis geſtat.

De rore cœli. 　　　Vrbanus. VII. qui fuit Archiepiſcopus Roſ-
　　　　　ſanenſis in Calabria,ubi mana colligitur.

Ex antiquitate Vrbis. Gregorius. XIIII.
Pia ciuitas in bello. 　Innocentius. IX.
Crux Romulea. 　　　Clemens. VIII.

Vndoſus uir.		Paſtor & nauta.
Gens peruerſa.	Animal rurale.	Flos florum.
In tribulatione pacis.	Roſa Vmbriæ.	De medietate lunæ.
Lilium & roſa.	Vrſus uelox.	De labore ſolis.
Iucunditas crucis.	Peregrin⁹apoſtolic⁹.	Gloria oliuæ.
Montium cuſtos.	Aquila rapax.	In pſecutione. extre-
Sydus olorum.	Canis & coluber.	ma S.R.E.ſedebit.
De flumine magno.	Vir religioſus.	Petrus Romanus, qui
Bellua inſatiabilis.	De balneis Ethruriæ.	paſcet oues in mul-
Pœnitentia glorioſa.	Crux de cruce.	tis tribulationibus:
Raſtrum in porta.	Lumen in cœlo.	quibus tranſactis ci-
Flores circundati.	Ignis ardens.	uitas ſepticollis di-
De bona religione.	Religio depopulata.	ruetur, & Iudex tre
Miles in bello.	Fides intrepida.	medus iudicabit po
Columna excelſa.	Paſtor angelicus.	pulum ſuum. Finis.

Quæ ad Pontifices adiecta,non ſunt ipſius Malachiæ , ſed R.P.F.
Alphonſi Giaconis,Ord.Prædicatoru,huius Prophetiæ interpretis.

3. Who Was St. Malachy?

Saint Malachy (1094 - 1148) was an Irish priest who accurately predicted 111 future Popes, including Pope Benedict XVI.

A second version of Malachy's predictions includes a final, *112th* leader of the Catholic Church, Peter the Roman (or Peter of Rome), who would witness the destruction of Rome.

Many people believe that the prophecies are the inspired words of Malachy. Others attribute them to the 15th century work of the Arnold de Wyon, who first published St. Malachy's noted *Prophecy of the Popes.*

Due to the details we know about Saint Malachy, we tend to believe they were the work of that saint.

Saint Malachy's life

Saint Malachy was baptized *Máel Máedóc ua Morgair* , also spelled Maolmhaodhog O' Morgair (Malachy O'Morgair). According to records, he was born in 1094 at Armagh, Ireland.

Armagh (in the Irish language: *Ard Mhacha*), originally named after an Irish goddess, has always been associated with power. It's nicknamed "the city of saints and scholars." It was the location of Saint Patrick's main church, built about 600 years before the birth of St. Malachy.

According to the *Annals of the Four Masters,* an early Irish history documented by monks:

> *Ard Mhacha* was founded by Saint Patrick, it having been granted to him by Daire, son of Finnchadh, son of Eoghan, son of Niallan.
>
> Twelve men were appointed by him for building the town.
>
> He ordered them, in the first place, to erect an archbishop's city there, and a church for monks, for

nuns, and for the other orders in general, for he perceived that it would be the head and chief of the churches of Ireland in general.

Brian Boru (941 - 1014), the most successful Irish king of his time, was buried at St. Patrick's church.

So, Saint Malachy was born to a noble family in a community filled with powerful, educated and very Christian people. Early in life, Malachy became noted for his spiritual gifts, including the ability to lay his hands on people and cure them almost instantly. According to stories, he could also levitate and -- as a clairvoyant -- perceive things that were distant (in space and time).

He may have been most famous for his gift of prophecy.

Divinely called to serve the church, Malachy was ordained as a priest in 1119, by Saint Cellach (Celsus), the Archbishop of Armagh. Malachy was 25 years old. Some suggest that he studied longer than usual, before requesting ordination.

And, even *after* his ordination, Malachy continued his studies. He spent nearly two years in Lismore, learning under the guidance of Saint Malchus.

Malachy soon attracted the attention of Saint Bernard of Clairvaux, France. Bernard encouraged Malachy and helped him establish the Cistercians (*Ordo Cisterciensis*) in Ireland. That's an order also known as the OSCO, or Trappists, as well as the *Bernardines* or the *White Monks,* since they dress in white. The order strictly follows *The Rule of Benedict,* including admonitions of *pax, ora et labora,* or "peace, pray, and work."

Note: Throughout many prophecies related to the last Pope -- as well as Pope Benedict XVI's history -- there seems to be a strong connection to St. Benedict. It's far beyond normal coincidence.

In 1132, after the death of Saint Cellach, Saint Malachy was appointed Archbishop of Armagh. However, due to conflicts within the Irish church, Malachy was unable to take possession of his See until 1135. He used his calling to restore order and discipline to the Catholic community, and apply the Roman Liturgy, including reforms of Pope Gregory VII.

In 1138, Malachy resigned as Archbishop of Armagh. Then, around 1139, during a two-year trip to the Vatican, Malachy had a vision. In it, he saw a long line of Popes, starting with the man who would succeed the current Pope, Innocent II. He transcribed his vision in Latin, giving short descriptions or mottoes to indicate the identity of each future Pope from the year 1143 to the end of the world.

Pope Innocent II, impressed by Malachy's spirituality and visions, named him as the Legate for Ireland. However, Malachy had hoped for additional permissions from Innocent II. Nevertheless, Malachy accepted his new calling and title with humility, and returned to Ireland.

While back in Ireland, Saint Malachy established and began to build Mellifont Abbey (in Irish, *An Mhainistir Mhór*, or "the big abbey). The site was not completed during Malachy's lifetime, but some of the structure remains at a site about ten miles northwest of Drogheda. By 1170, Mellifont Abbey was the home of over 100 monks and 300 lay brothers. It became the model of all future Cistercian abbeys built in Ireland.

Then, Saint Malachy received a very personal vision. It predicted the date of his own death.

In 1148, wanting to visit the Pope one final time, Saint Malachy began his journey. Unfortunately, he only reached Clairvaux Abbey in France. Malachy died on the predicted day, November 2nd, 1148, and at the predicted time.

Saint Bernard sat with Saint Malachy as he died, and later wrote a book about his life.

In 1199, Malachy was the first Irish saint canonized. His feast day is November 3rd, the day after the celebration of

All Souls Day.

4. Who Was Arnold Wyon and Did He Write Malachy's Prophecies?

Arnold Wyon -- also spelled Arnold de Wyon, Arnold de Wion, Arnoldo VVion, Arnoldo Wion, and Arnould Wion -- was born in 1554 and died around 1610. He was a Benedictine monk. It also seems like he was *fascinated* by history and old books. And, he was given access to all those random repositories of old Vatican documents, scattered around Rome. So, what happened next might not be a surprise.

Wyon found, transcribed or copied -- and in 1595 was the first to publish -- Malachy's *Prophecy of the Popes* in Wyon's book, *Lignum Vitae*. Part of title page is shown, below.

LIGNVM VITAE,

Ornamentum, & Decus Ecclefiæ,

CONTINENS

TRES POSTERIORES LIBROS.

In quibus,

Totius Sanctifs. Religionis DIVI BENEDICTI Viri, Sanctitate, ac Principatu clari defcribuntur, & Fructus qui per eos S. R. E. accefferunt, fufiffimè explicantur.

AVCTORE

D. ARNOLDO VVION, BELGA, DVACENS

Monacho S. Benedicti de Mantua, Ord. Diui BENEDICTI Nigrorum, Congregationis Cafinenfis, aliàs S. fultinæ de Padua.

Acceffit Informatio ad Stemmata illa depingenda, quæ in folio fevarato continentur.

Arnold Wyon has been described as a Flemish (or Belgian) Benedictine monk who lived and wrote at Monte Cassino.

Monte Cassino is a rocky hill about 130 kilometres

(81 mi) southeast of Rome, Italy, and the site of an early temple to Apollo. Around 529, St. Benedict of Nursia (480 - 547) established his first monastery, the source of the Benedictine Order, at that location.

The area was mostly pagan at the time, but St. Benedict's first act was to smash the sculpture of Apollo. Then, he destroyed the temple's altar. After that, St. Benedict decided to reuse the temple building, dedicating it to Saint Martin. Where the altar to Apollo had stood, St. Benedict built a small chapel and dedicated it to Saint John the Baptist.

It didn't make him popular in the neighborhood.

Despite the monastery's difficult beginnings, the site flourished from 529 to about 581. Then, it was sacked by Lombards. The monks fled, taking the the body of St Benedict -- who'd died about 30 years earlier -- to Fleury (the modern Saint-Benoit-sur-Loire) near Orleans, France.

Eventually, the monastery was rebuilt, but sacked and destroyed again, this time in 884, by Saracens. (It sounds like Monte Cassino wasn't a charmed location for *any* religious building.)

The monastery was rebuilt yet *again,* and reached its peak in the 11th century, but then it was badly damaged by an earthquake in 1349.

Undaunted, Pope John XXII put the site under protection as a cathedral, and in 1505 the monastery merged with the monastery of St. Justina of Padua, and began to recover some of its former glory.

That's the era when Arnold Wyon was there, and compiled his 1595 book that included the first known publication of St. Malachy's prophecies about future Popes.

Finally, the site was sacked by Napoleon's troops in 1799. I think the church pretty much gave up on it, at least for awhile.

Starting with the dissolution of the Italian monasteries in 1866, Monte Cassino became a national monument, and a storehouse for valuable church documents. By then, Monte Cassino's literary treasures -- overlooked by looters more interested in gold and jewels -- were all that remained from the monastery's early days.

That's when the story gets interesting. You see, despite looting by the Germans in World War II, *most of the documents were salvaged* and -- under pressure by the Pope -- delivered to the Vatican.

However, as many as 15 crates of valuable documents and art were withheld by the Germans and delivered as a birthday present to Goring in December, 1943.

In other words, **Malachy's *Prophecy of the Popes* may still exist**, either at the Vatican or in an undetermined site along with other property held by Goring. One possible location was Berchtesgaden.

But, let's take a look at Friar Wyon. He was a man with eclectic interests. We know he was an admirer of two people.

One was Bede. Wyon quoted an epitaph for Bede, *"Beda, Dei famulus, monachorum nobile sidus, finibus e terrae profuit Ecclesiae,"* loosely translated as "Bede, the servant of God, and a noble monk of the stars, and all the territory of the Church, lived a useful life." We think Wyon liked the "useful life" tribute, and aspired to do the same, himself.

Wyon also admired Johannes Trithemius (1462 - 1516), a Benedictine Abbot of Sponheim.

However, Trithemius was also an occultist and aspiring magician associated with the original tales of *Dr. Faustus.* Trithemius also associated with Heinrich Cornelius Agrippa (1486–1535) and Paracelsus (1493–1541).

As you might expect, Trithemius was censured for his work with magic. He just couldn't seem to stay away from it. In fact, his most famous work, *Steganographia* seemed to be about using spirits to communicate across long distances. The three-volume set included references to Agrippa and

John Dee, and it was placed on the *Index Librorum Prohibitorum* -- the "banned book" list -- in 1609 and not removed until 1900.

In other words, Wyon had a background in history *and* he was an admirer of occult studies. He may even have dabbled in alchemy.

With access to Vatican documents, Wyon was the *perfect person* to work with Saint Malachy's prophecies. Also, not to get too woo-woo about this, but... well, Monte Cassino's history may have made it an ideal place to interpret -- or perhaps construct -- the St. Malachy document. (Today, a site so often sacked and destroyed, and then hit with an earthquake... we'd call it *haunted,* if not *cursed.*)

Three theories about Malachy's *Prophecy of the Popes*

At least three theories suggest the truth about the origins of Saint Malachy's prophecies.

Theory One

Saint Malachy really *did* predict the 111 (or 112) Popes that would follow Innocent II.

If this is true, there are a couple of questions about Wyon's work.

First, did Wyon copy *all* of Malachy's predictions? Or, did Wyon get tired (or was he rushed) after copying 111 from the list? In a moment of impatience, did he throw the final prediction -- the Petrus Romanus (Peter of Rome) lines -- into his book, thinking it was "good enough"?

Maybe he expected someone else to pick up Malachy's work where Wyon left off.

The problem is, for all of Wyon's writing, *he didn't leave behind a diary,* or any hints about the thoroughness of his work. So, a lot of this is open to conjecture.

Theory Two

The Saint Malachy prophecies were created around 1595, from scratch.

Many people support this theory. They claim that the writing style is more 16th century than 12th century. They also point to the absolute accuracy of the predictions up through 1595, but less reliable information -- at least 70 - 93% accuracy, depending on the analyst's standards -- for Popes after 1595. (Even 70% accuracy is remarkable, given the centuries those predictions cover.)

If this is true, the question is: Who actually made the predictions? Was it John Dee, a contemporary of Arnold Wyon, or someone else altogether?

Several scholars -- including John Hogue, author of *The Last Pope, Revisited* -- seem to believe that the writing style, choice of (Irish) Saint Malachy as the "source" of the information, and the details of the prophecies indicate an Irish author with a knowledge of medieval Latin, with reference materials from the Vatican.

However, if you're going to create that kind of fiction, wouldn't you choose someone like Saint Patrick as the prophet? He was more famous, lived longer, traveled more widely, and had already written about the "end times" or the end of the world.

As recorded in the 1827 book, Irish Antiquarian Researches, volume 2:

> *These are the three prayers of Patrick, as they were delivered to us by the Hibernians, entreating that all should be received on the day of judgment, if we should repent even in the last days of our life.*
>
> *1. That he should not be shut up in hell.*
>
> *2. That barbarian nations should never have the rule over us.*
>
> *3. That no one shall conquer us, that is the Scots, before seven years previous to the day of judgment, because seven years before the judgment we shall be destroyed in the sea, this is*

the third.

Likewise, the Irish saint, Columbkille (St. Columba), prophecied the end times:

> *I concede a favour to them without exception,*
> *and St Patrick also did concede the same;*
> *that seven years before the last day,*
> *the sea shall submerge Eirin by one inundation.*

So, creating Saint Malachy as the source of the *Prophecy of the Popes* is possible, but a little unlikely.

The original "Malachy" document might exist. Though we want to believe the story as originally told -- even if Malachy's original work *could* be found and analyzed -- it *might* reveal 16th century ink on authentic parchment, or other writing materials consistent with Malachy's era. Or, in the 16th century, forging old documents might not have been that sophisticated.

Theory Three

The Saint Malachy document was real, but the information was updated as it was copied by Arnold Wyon.

In this version of the story, Arnold Wyon *did* find St. Malachy's predictions among Vatican documents. However, to enhance their value, he may have "improved" some of the prophecies so they more clearly indicated the Popes who had been elected. For the future Popes, unless Wyon (or a confederate) had the gift of prophecy, Wyon had to rely on the Saint Malachy verses, exactly as written.

Studying Saint Malachy's *Prophecy of the Popes,* it's impossible to tell which of those explanations fits best.

Our consensus is: Some or all of the predictions were real, and came from Saint Malachy. Whether they *all* did, or were transcribed by Wyon, *verbatim...* that remains to be seen.

5. Portraits, Crypt Space, the 666 Tiara, and Other Legends

The following are the most popular questions asked, and our answers to them.

Was Pope Benedict XVI the last Pope?

If Malachy's predictions are correct, Benedict XVI was probably the last Pope. He's certainly the last on Malachy's *regular* list.

The 112th possible leader of the Catholic Church -- *Petrus Romanus* -- wasn't described in the same terms as the other 111. That might be important. It could be a huge clue.

Whatever *else* explains the change, it's as if a very dark vision was in front of Malachy as he talked about that possible outcome.

Sure, that 112th entry might have been added by Wyon. The point is, everything from 1595 (when Wyon published the work) to the present has been eerily accurate. So, no matter *who* made up the entries, we tend to take them seriously.

Though Pope Francis was elected after Benedict retired, he might be nothing more than a figurehead. That seems unlikely, but we're watching carefully. We take the St. Malachy prophecy seriously.

As others have suggested, Benedict may have been the last Pope *worth listing*. Since Malachy's list included several antipopes... that's saying a *lot*.

What's the legend about space at the Vatican for just one more Pope?

There are several variations on this kind of legend. There are stories like these connected with the headquarters of almost every major religion, and similar tales about the White House in the USA, the Kremlin, and so on. Dan Brown and Brad Meltzer are just a couple of writers whose work features some of those elements.

The main Vatican stories are interesting because both suggest that space has been allocated for just one more Pope.

Two tales relate to the walls of St. Paul's Church, and the Papal portraits displayed there. One rumor claimed that there was room for just one Pope's portrait after John Paul II's. That's been discredited.

The other -- and more widely accepted story-- is that there's room for just one portrait after Benedict XVI's. So far, no one has denied that.

The second story is that the crypt of St. Peter's Basilica has room for two more Popes. One will be Benedict XVI. The other will be Pope Francis.

Since a Pope is supposed to be appointed for life, is the next Pope going to be a real Pope?

Interesting question. Our answer is yes, since it has been declared that the Pope can resign. Pope Francis is *considered* a real Pope.

What happens to the Catholic Church under his reign -- and any "Popes" that follow -- remains to be seen.

What old Italian proverb requires two living Popes? How does that fit prophecies about the Pope?

The most likely "old Italian proverb" is this:

> "When the White Pope and the Black Pope shall die during the same night, then there will dawn upon the Christian nations the Great White Day."

Pope Francis is known for favoring the traditional, simple, black cassock of his order, the Jesuits. So, he might be the "Black Pope."

Pope Benedict XVI startled many people by announcing that, in addition to remaining a Pope, he'd continue to wear his white cassock. So, he might be the "White Pope."

So, if -- by sheer coincidence or to fulfill prophecy -- Benedict XVI and Francis I died on the same night, that would match the legend.

But, there's room for other interpretations of "Peter the Roman" as well as the "black" significance. They could refer to a family name, a hometown motto, a crest or coat of arms related to the individual, and so on.

Yet another legend claims that the last Pope will be from a Jewish family. We look forward to seeing whether or not that is fulfilled.

What about the 666 message on the Pope's tiara?

This story seemed to begin in 1915, when the following appeared in "Our Sunday Visitor," a popular Catholic magazine.

> *Q. What are the letters on the Pope's crown and what do they signify if anything?*
>
> *A. The letters on the Pope's mitre are these: Vicarius Filii Dei, which is a Latin for Vicar of the Son of God.*

That set off a furor, as some people -- especially critics of Catholicism -- took the letters and interpreted them as Roman numerals. Of course, some of the letters couldn't be used as Roman numerals, so they were dropped out, though the letter U was changed to a V.

This left: V+I+C+I+V+I+L+I+I+D+I. This computes as: 5+1+100+1+5+1+50+1+1+500+1 = *666*

The author of the article in *Our Sunday Visitor* not only withdrew his response in 1914, he did so again in 1915.

> However, the conspiracy theorist were not to be denied. Finally, in 1922, the magazine published this statement: "The Pope claims to be the vicar of the Son of God, while the Latin words for this designation are not inscribed, as anti-Catholics maintain, on the Pope's tiara."

To this day, many people still believe that the original answer is the correct one. Cue the *Twilight Zone* music.

Why would *anyone* -- especially a Pope -- want to wear 666 on his head, except as a Halloween costume in *very* poor taste?

All kidding aside, even if it does say *Vicarius Filii Dei* on the tiara, the 666 computation using letters as Roman numerals... it seems like a stretch.

Was Pope John Paul I poisoned?

This rumor persists, partly due to the brief time he held office: about a month. Other questions have been raised about that Pope's death, including speculation fictionalized in Dan Brown's book, *Angels and Demons*.

We have no additional insights about Pope John Paul I's death. We're sure you can find many theories online. Some are more sinister than others. Illuminati, the Mafia, rival cardinals... there seems to be no *limit* to possible villains and co-conspirators in this mystery.

However, John Paul I wasn't the only Pope to die quickly after election.

- Marcellus II (1555) died after just 22 days as Pope; Malachy's description for him was "Bread-corn, suddenly perishing."
- Pope Leo XI (1605) caught a cold and died from complications just 27 days after his reign began. Malachy's description: "A man gone as soon as a wave."

What about the Third (and possible Fourth) Secret of Fatima? Do they really talk about Satan taking control of the Vatican?

It seems to be generally acknowledged that we received only part of the Third Secret, and the missing part -- or alternative version -- describes the Apocalypse and the fate of the Catholic Church.

Here's the content of the Third Secret, as revealed by the Vatican (emphasis added):

The third part of the secret revealed at the Cova da Iria-Fátima, on 13 May 1917.

I write in obedience to you, my God, who command me to do so through his Excellency the Bishop of Leiria and through your Most Holy Mother and mine.

After the two parts which I have already explained, at the left of Our Lady and a little above, we saw an Angel with a flaming sword in his left hand; flashing, it gave out flames that looked as though they would set the world on fire; but they died out in contact with the splendour that Our Lady radiated towards him from her right hand: pointing to the earth with his right hand, the Angel cried out in a loud voice: 'Penance, Penance, Penance!'.

And we saw in an immense light that is God: 'something similar to how people appear in a mirror when they pass in front of it' a Bishop dressed in White 'we had the impression that it was the Holy Father'.

Other Bishops, Priests, men and women Religious going up a steep mountain, at the top of which there was a big Cross of rough-hewn trunks as of a cork-tree with the bark; before reaching there the Holy Father passed through a big city half in ruins and half trembling with halting step, afflicted with pain and sorrow, he prayed for the souls of the corpses he met on his way; **having reached the top of the mountain, on his knees at the foot of the big Cross he was killed by a group of soldiers who fired bullets and arrows at him,** *and in the same way there died one after another the other Bishops, Priests, men and women Religious, and various lay people of different ranks and positions.*

Beneath the two arms of the Cross there were two Angels each with a crystal aspersorium in his

> *hand, in which they gathered up the blood of the*
> *Martyrs and with it sprinkled the souls that were*
> *making their way to God.*

However, that may not be the *real* Third Secret, or it may be just part of it. In fact, some credible sources have said that there were *two* versions of the Third Secret.

On one of Art Bell's shows, Father Malachi Martin (1921 - 1999) shared his views about that secret. A caller said that he'd heard from a Jesuit priest that the Third Secret included references to the last pope being under the control of Satan. He asked if Father Martin could confirm that. Father Martin said, "Yes, it sounds as if they were reading, or being told, the text of the Third Secret. But it's sufficiently vague to make one hesitate — it sounds like it."

Howard Dee, former Philippine ambassador to the Vatican, said that **Cardinal Ratzinger (now Pope Benedict XVI) had personally confirmed that the messages of Our Lady of Akita (Japan) and Fatima are "essentially the same."**

The Akita prophecy, in part, contains the following:

> "The work of the devil will infiltrate even into the
> Church in such a way that one will see cardinals
> opposing cardinals, bishops against bishops. The
> priests who venerate Me will be scorned and
> opposed by their confreres ... churches and altars
> sacked; **the Church will be full of those who
> accept compromises and the demon will
> press many priests and consecrated souls to
> leave the service of the Lord.**"

It presents a very dark future for the Catholic Church.

Likewise, Cardinal Mario Ciappi was quoted, "**In the Third Secret it is foretold, among other things, that the great apostasy in the Church will begin at the top.**" Cardinal Ciappi (1909 - 1996) served as personal theologian to five Popes between 1955 to 1989.

Assuming that quote is accurate, it echoes another quote from Lucia herself, who wrote down the secrets.

Reportedly, she said that it was "in the Gospels and in the Apocalypse." She mentioned Revelations (Apocalypse) chapters 8 to 13, a range that includes *Revelations 12:4,* the chapter and verse cited by Pope John Paul II in his homily in Fatima on 13 May 2000:

> *And his tail drew the third part of the stars of heaven, and did cast them to the earth: and the dragon stood before the woman which was ready to be delivered, for to devour her child as soon as it was born.*

Rather than reinvent the wheel, we recommend a book that's free, online, called *The Secret Still Hidden,* and that book's *Epilogue,* also online. They're written by Catholic attorney and president of the American Catholic Lawyers Association, Christopher A. Ferrara. If you like dark, somewhat frightening (okay... *terrifying*) views of the future, his books are worth reading.

Was Pope Benedict XVI in league with the Freemasons? Were other Popes connected with Freemasonry?

We've seen photos of Pope Benedict XVI exchanging Masonic-style handshakes with several men. There's no denying that distinctive gesture. We'd also argue that, given the Pope's arthritis, he might not always be capable of a full, *non*-Masonic handshake.

Either might explain the fingers-to-the-mid-palm sign of greeting.

On the other hand (no pun intended), we've seen compelling evidence "hiding in plain sight" to suggest that something darker has invaded the Vatican. Pope Paul VI (1963 - 1978) chose his words carefully when he referenced "the smoke of Satan which has entered the Sanctuary."

Father Malachi Martin was deeply involved in investigations related to Satanic influences in the Catholic Church. The occult connections to the unsolved murder of Father Alfred Kunz (1931 -1998) -- a friend of Martin's, investigating sexual abuse in the church in Illinois -- still raise eyebrows. Many people, including Martin, link the occult to Freemasonry, and then show ties to the Vatican.

How deep are those ties? We're not sure. It's a deep and dark topic to explore, with global ties that could fuel an endless stream of Dan Brown novels.

We acknowledge evidence that *seems* to connect the Vatican with Freemasonry. We also know the Catholic Church's stance on Freemasonry, as stated by EWTN: "Freemasonry is incompatible with the Catholic faith."

And, in that same article, EWTN says,

> "Historically, one of Masonry's primary objectives has been the destruction of the Catholic Church; this is especially true of Freemasonry as it has existed in certain European countries."

Father Martin would have agreed, wholeheartedly.

It's not our cup of tea, but others have shared their Masonic/Vatican-related evidence in books, interviews, and online. If you start with the writing of Father Martin, you'll find enough leads to keep you busy for years.

Was Pope Benedict XVI the victim of politics or conspiracy?

Those rumors are likely to continue. They're built, in part, on speculation that -- as the oldest man named Pope in the past 300 years -- he wasn't expected to live more than a few years. Some suggest that he was there to take the fall for bad behavior by the clergy, and weather what the church hoped would be a short-lived storm.

We think it's mean and insulting to consider Benedict XVI in that light.

However, there can be no denying that his reign has been during a *very* turbulent episode in the history of the Catholic Church. Newspaper headlines and political disagreements have been unavoidable.

In the coming months and years, we're sure additional stories, rumors, and theories will come to light.

No doubt, there are lessons to be learned from the foibles and shortcomings of everyone, including those who achieve levels of status and responsibility in religion and government. No one is immune from mistakes.

For now, we choose to take Pope Benedict XVI's explanation at face value, and we wish him a relaxed and health-restoring retirement, and many years of happiness in the privacy of his new home.

6. Antipopes, False Popes, and Pope Joan

An **antipope** (Latin: *antipapa*) is a person who -- outside of the most accepted election in Rome -- gains at least moderate support in his claim as the real Pope.

Most of these events occurred between the 3rd and mid-15th century. It seemed to be a regional competition. It's as if *ad hoc* "Popes" were endorsed by countries, kings, and religious communities. And, in a world not as connected as ours, it might have worked. Rome probably seemed light years away to people in other countries.

Then, things got *really* political. During the 11th century, Holy Roman Emperors were trying to maintain power, but that power wasn't always distinct from the church. (Things didn't get really ugly until the 16th century, when Henry VIII turned state v. church power struggles into a *big* issue.)

Meanwhile, back in the 11th century, some "emperors" chose their *own* Popes , and -- with or without Rome's support -- declared each of their candidates the *real* Pope. But, things were going to get worse before they got better.

The Great Western Schism began in 1378, when the French cardinals elected Clement VII as Pope. The French said that the Roman election of Pope Urban VI wasn't valid, and they refused to support him. Other people weren't happy with Clement VII... but they weren't entirely pleased with Urban VI, either.

This led to a three-way split in the church:

- The Roman line, where Urban VI was Pope.
- The Avignon (France) line, where Clement VII was Pope.
- The Pisan line (Pisa, Italy), where Alexander V was appointed as the third Pope during the same time period.

Yes, there were two countries and three Popes, all at the

same time. Nobody was going to back down. Not for *years*.

About 40 stress- and conflict-filled years later, in May 1415, the Catholic Church decided was time to end the schism. To bring this about:

The Council of Constance deposed John XXIII of the Pisan line. Yep, end of the line for the Pisan Popes. (It's interesting that *another* Pope chose the John XXIII name, in the 20th century.)

- Pope Gregory XII of the Roman line "resigned" in July 1415. According to stories, he didn't have much choice. We're not saying they made him an offer he couldn't refuse, but he knew he was out of the running for Pope, either way.
- The Council formally deposed Benedict XIII of Avignon in 1417, but -- unlike Gregory XII -- Benedict XIII of Avignon refused to resign. Lacking local support, he fled to Aragon, where he was treated well and lived as "Pope" until his death in 1423.
- Pope Martin V was officially elected and sustained by the Roman Catholic Church in 1417. It was an uneasy agreement, but everyone seemed ready to "make nice," at least until 1420 when Pope Martin V initiated the Hussite Wars. Martin continued to spark conflicts, and in 1431, he died from a fit of apoplexy.

Martin V was followed by Pope Eugene IV, dubbed "heavenly she-wolf" in Saint Malachy's prophecy.

Eugene had won Papal election by being a smart politician. Before the vote, Eugene promised -- in writing -- to give the cardinals one-half of all the revenues of the Church.

He also agreed to actually listen to them before making spiritual and temporal decisions for the church. He still had a difficult time of it, and on his deathbed, he said he regretted ever leaving his monastery.

It was a difficult era. Eugene's successor was Nicholas V, so universally disliked that, a year before his death in 1453, he had to put down a rabid Roman conspiracy to overthrow his power.

Nicholas V was followed by Callixtus III. He may have been feeble, but he knew how to hold the church together. If his name sounds unfamiliar, you might recognize his birth name: Alfons de Borja. He was the first of the Borgias to be elected Pope.

We kind of *like* Callixtus III, if only because he gave Joan of Arc a new trial (though she'd been dead more than 20 years) and she was posthumously vindicated.

Anyway...

The following list includes *most* antipopes, but not all of them. They're listed by the years in which they attempted to reign, followed by each person's English name as Pope, and then the Latin version of the Pope's name. Pope's names with an asterisk were adjusted to accommodate the sequence of names of *accepted* Popes, in hopes of avoiding confusion.

Note: In reviewing Saint Malachy's list of Popes, you'll see many antipopes among his predictions.

Antipopes

c. 200   Natalius / Natalius
217–235   Saint Hippolytus / Hippolytus
251–258   Novatian / Novatianus
355–365   Felix II* / Felix secundus
366–367   Ursicinus / Ursicinus
418–419   Eulalius / Papa Eulalius
498–499, 501–506   Laurentius   /   Papa Laurentius
530   Dioscorus / Papa Dioscurus
687   Theodore / Papa Theodorus
687   Paschal (I) / Papa Paschalis
767–768   Constantine II / Papa Constantinus secundus
768   Philip / Papa Philippus
844   John VIII / Papa Joannes octavus
855   Anastasius III Bibliothecarius ("librarian") / Papa

Anastasius tertius
903–904   Christopher / Papa Christophorus

963 - 964   Leo VIII (He was an *official* Pope 964 - 965)
974 , 984–985   Boniface VII / Papa Bonifacius septimus
997–998   John XVI* / Papa Joannes sextus decimus
1012   Gregory VI / Papa Gregorius sextus
1058–1059   Benedict X* / Papa Benedictus decimus
1061–1064   Honorius II / Papa Honorius secundus
1080, 1084–1100   Clement III / Papa Clemens tertius
1100–1101   Theodoric / Papa Theodoricus
1101   Adalbert or Albert / Papa Adalbertus
1105–1111   Sylvester IV / Papa Sylvester quartus
1118–1121   Gregory VIII / Papa Gregorius octavus
1124   Celestine II / Papa Cœlestinus secundus
1130–1138   Anacletus II / Papa Anacletus secundus
1138   Victor IV / Papa Victor quartus   (personal name: Gregorio Conti)
1159–1164   Victor IV / Papa Victor quartus   (personal name: Ottavio di Montecelio)
1164–1168   Paschal III / Papa Paschalis tertius
1168–1178   Callixtus III / Papa Callixtus tertius
1179–1180   Innocent III / Papa Innocentius tertius
1328–1330   Nicholas V / Papa Nicolaus quintus
1378–1394   Clement VII / Papa Clemens septimus
1394–1423   Benedict XIII / Papa Benedictus tertius decimus
1409–1410   Alexander V* / Papa Alexander quintus
1410–1415   John XXIII / Papa Joannes vicesimus tertius
1423–1429   Clement VIII / Papa Clemens octavus
1424–1429   Benedict XIV / Papa Benedictus quartus decimus
1430–1437   Benedict XIV / Papa Benedictus quartus decimus
1439–1449   Felix V / Papa Fœlix quintus

False Popes

A **false pope** is similar to an antipope, but he lacks sufficient support to be a serious threat to the elected Pope in Rome. From earliest to modern times, many people have claimed that they're the only *real* Pope. The list would be very long.

These categories do *not* include religious organizations and divisions that may or may not consider themselves part of the Catholic community in general, but no longer accept the Pope in Rome as their spiritual leader. Reasons vary from doctrinal matters to Papal succession disputes, and a wide range of other concerns.

Pope Joan

Pope Joan is one of several legendary Popes with questionable histories. Despite that, her stories linger.

Pope Joan's story is one of the most popular, but it has many variations. The following is one of them.

Joan's story first appeared in 1250, in the *Chronica universalis Mettensis*, as told by Dominican historian Jean Pierier of Mailly, also known as Jean de Mailly. Here is that story:

> Concerning a certain Pope or rather female Pope, who is not set down in the list of popes or Bishops of Rome, because she was a woman who disguised herself as a man and became, by her character and talents, a curial secretary, then a Cardinal and finally Pope.

> One day, while mounting a horse, she gave birth to a child. Immediately, by Roman justice, she was bound by the feet to a horse's tail and dragged and stoned by the people for half a league, and, where she died, there she was buried, and at the place is written: *'Petre, Pater Patrum, Papisse Prodito Partum'* [Oh Peter, Father of Fathers, Betray the childbearing of the woman Pope].

> At the same time, the four-day fast called the "fast of the female Pope" was first established.

Here's one of many more *modern* versions of the tale:

> In the ninth century, a woman named Joan was born in Mainz, Germany. Early in her adult life, she found life as a woman too constrained. She took a

lover and, together, they moved to Athens where Joan studied the classics. However, to have access to some libraries, she had to pretend she was a man. After some time, she moved to England and changed her name to John Anglicus, continuing her pretense.

Finally, as enthusiastic historian and teacher, "John" traveled to Rome. There, "he" became such a popular lecturer, he was elected as a cardinal in the Catholic Church. Then, when Pope Leo IV died, Joan was so well liked, she -- as John Anglicus -- was almost unanimously elected as Pope.

Everything was fine until, after two years at the Vatican, she became pregnant. One day, while riding a horse through the streets of Rome, Joan went into labor. She slid off the horse and stumbled to a nearby lane, once called *Via Sacra* or "Sacred Lane."

Note: Today, it's called *Via S. Giovanni,* more popularly known as the "shunned street" because of its connection with that embarrassing episode in church history. It's between the Colosseum and St Clement's church.

Of course, Pope Joan's secret could not be concealed, and -- with horror -- the Holy See realized that they'd elected a woman Pope. In one version of the story (recounted in the 13th century), Joan was put to death.

Another version says that Joan was deposed as Pope, served her penance, and lived long enough to see her son -- possibly named Stephen or Guido -- named Bishop of Ostia.

Circumstantial evidence supports the idea that she was a real person, and became Pope.

A late-14th-century edition of the Roman guidebook, *Mirabilia Urbis Romae*, states that Joan's remains are buried at St. Peter's, among the other Popes. Also, when a long series of busts of past Popes was made for the Duomo of Siena. The busts included one of the female Pope, named as "Johannes VIII, Foemina de Anglia." It was placed between the busts of Popes Leo IV and Benedict III.

In the early 15th-century, Jan Hus was trial for heresy, related to the infallibility of the Pope. Hus made many statements in his defense. All but one were contradicted by the judges, and declared blasphemous. The *one and only statement* that was not challenged by his judges was related to Pope Joan.

Hus said, "Many times have the Popes fallen into sin and error, for instance when Joan was elected Pope, who was a woman."

(In the actual records, he may have referred to her as Agnes, another name -- perhaps a "code name" at the time -- for Pope Joan. According to some stories, her statue is "hiding in plain sight" in Rome, labeled as *Agnes*. However, there was a Saint Agnes of Rome who lived in the third century. She's the patron saint of young girls.)

According to reports, no one in the court -- including over 30 cardinals and over 200 bishops -- challenged or disagreed with Hus on that one point about a past, female Pope. (Unfortunately, Hus lost his case on the other points, and was burned at the stake as a heretic.)

7. Matching Popes and Prophecy

How are Popes matched to Malachy's predictions?

In his book, *The Last Pope, Revisited,* author John Hogue has provided 11 ways to determine if a prediction matches a particular Papal candidate or Pope. They include:

- Connect the Pope's Christian name to the prediction.
- Look for events at the relevant time, and how closely they match the election of the new Pope.
- Check the geographic locations associated with the Pope, including their historical names and descriptive references.
- Examine relevant coats of arms for symbols or phrases that connect with the predictions.

How many Popes *really* match St. Malachy's description? Aren't some of them a stretch?

Those questions have been asked for centuries. In 1746, James Ware published his comments about St. Malachy's work. Ware said, "This Prophecy of Malachy is looked upon as a most absurd, impertinent forgery, by the best Popish criticks [sic], and has been demonstrated to be so."

However, the more access we have to historical records, the more accurate the predictions seem. It's impressive.

Out of 112 predictions, about 75 of them are *absolutely* accurate. However, they pre-date 1595, when the first known copy of St. Malachy's prophecies were published. So, if the work is a fake, you'd *expect* complete accuracy regarding past events. Revisionist history is a wonderful thing.

Saint Malachy's predictions' credibility rests in the *remaining* predictions, which occurred *after* the 1595 publication of *Prophecy of the Popes.*

35 predictions since then have -- so far -- been remarkably

accurate. Most historians rate them at 75% - 95% correct, depending on how strict your standards are. (The 75% figure requires the verse to match one, and *only* one, likely candidate for Pope. At the 95% end of things, there may be some "Sure, close enough" judgment calls.)

Did any Popes *not* match Malachy's predictions?

At least four predictions were either too vague or seemed not to have a precise connection with just one candidate for Pope, who was *also* the one elected.

But -- to be fair -- we have so many more resources to research each Papal candidate, those four apparent "errors" may yet turn out to be accurate.

While researching this book, we found considerable information that -- until recently -- had not been readily available to people conducting routine research. For example, we've found a couple of clues to indicate where the original Saint Malachy document might be. That's pretty close to awesome.

In addition, more advanced numerological and numerical studies may indicate which interpretation of the 112th prediction is the most correct.

Have some of the so-called "predictions" been rewritten so they more closely match the related Pope?

No. You can see the original pages from the 1595 book, as well as interpretations and translations of the mottoes.

Not only were none changed, but some went *far* out on a limb from the very beginning. If no Pope had matched the description, it would be obvious there was no match. (In an earlier chapter, we mentioned the "snaky man" description. Seriously, you can't *make up* that kind of nickname and have it turn out accurate.)

What about the antipopes? Which ones were they? Do their inclusions prove that the list is contrived or even fake?

In our chapter about the antipopes, "Antipopes, False

Popes, and Pope Joan," we've listed the most notable men elected Pope by various schismatic factions of the Catholic Church. It's difficult to identify which of them were merely aspirants to the position, and which were -- by many standards -- truly *called* as Pope, whether or not the full church and Holy See accepted them.

And, in most cases, it all depended on where you lived. The French supported one Pope and the Romans declared another one the only "true" Pope. Travel must have been interesting. We bet a lot of people just vaguely said, "the Pope," figuring it was safest not to mention a specific name. Discretion was the rule of the day.

As far as we're concerned, whether those men were formally recognized as Popes -- or whether they were simply among the most popular claimants to the title -- there's no reason for them *not* to be included in Saint Malachy's list. At no time did he declare the list official. He was merely documenting a startling vision that he had, around 1139.

What does the Catholic Church say about Malachy's prophecies?

Generally, the church ignores or dismisses prophecies such as Saint Malachy's. The Malachy predictions are especially problematic because there is no real provenance for them, and enough irregularities to question if they even existed before the 1550s. (See our chapter, "Who Was Arnold Wyon and Did He Write Malachy's Prophecies?")

Some claim that the accuracy of Saint Malachy's predictions are *so* threatening, the church dares not acknowledge them. That's pretty dramatic, but hey... it might be true.

Either way, it's become obvious that the College of Cardinals not only *know* about the Saint Malachy prophecies, but at least a few of them may take the predictions -- or their influence on others -- very seriously. Maybe too seriously.

For example, there's a 1958 story (not fully documented)

that Cardinal Spellman of New York was so eager to be identified as the "Shepherd and Sailor" (prediction #107), he hired a boat, filled it with sheep, and sailed it up and down the Tiber River for the other cardinals to see him.

It didn't help. John XXIII was elected, instead.

Then there's the issue of the burial of John Paul II (*De Labore Sulis,* the Labor of the Sun or a Solar Eclipse), who was born on the day of a solar eclipse and was buried on the day of a solar eclipse.

If the church had wanted to discredit the Saint Malachy predictions, they *could* have moved the burial date ahead or back, to avoid the coincidence of the eclipse.

That's baffling. We're not sure what to think about it, but it's cool that the prophecy was *that* accurate.

Were any Popes elected because of a connection with a Malachy prophecy?

Because the Pope's selection takes place in private, away from observers, we can't be sure that the Malachy document *wasn't* considered or discussed.

In fact, if the story about Cardinal Spellman *is* true -- and we're not sure it is -- maybe predictions attributed to Saint Malachy *are* taken seriously. At least by some people. With boats. And sheep.

Did Joachim de Fiore (or de Flora) predict the last Pope?

No. Generally, Joachim de Fiore's predicted an ultimately utopian world -- the Age of the Holy Spirit -- that began to emerge in the year 1260. It followed the Age of the Father, corresponding to the Old Testament years, and the Age of the Son, which extended from the birth of Christ to the year 1260. (Ref: Rev. 11:3 and 12:6.)

We really *like* his faith in mankind. After all, the 13th century was when internal church politics was practically a runaway train, heading directly for the Great Western Schism.

During Fiore's lifetime (1135 - 1202), he was generally regarded as a visionary. He was well-known for his passionate and optimistic views of the Book of Revelations. Some say that Richard the Lionheart wanted to meet with Fiore for theological discussions before leaving for the Third Crusade. Fiore was definitely the go-to guy if you wanted to feel like everything's going to work out well, in the end.

Some said that miracles took place at Fiore's tomb after his death. Dante Alighieri confirmed this. Though never officially beatified, Joachim de Fiore is still venerated as a *beatus* on May 29.

Many later works attributed to him have been discredited. We kind of like that. After all, he was such a wonderful man, there's no need to embellish his history or make up prophecies.

Also, the connection between Fiore's predictions and Barack Obama's 2008 campaign speeches have been dismissed as a hoax. But, it's nice to think that Fiore is still so present in some people's thoughts.

Did St. John Bosco predict the last Pope?

Maybe. In the May 1862 vision of St. John Bosco, described in *Forty Dreams of John Bosco,* we see the following:

> "Suddenly the Pope falls gravely wounded. Immediately, those who are with him run to help him and they lift him up. A second time the Pope is struck, he falls again and dies. A shout of victory and joy rings out amongst the enemies; from their ships an unspeakable mockery arises.

> "But hardly is the Pontiff dead than another takes his place. The pilots, having met together, have elected the Pope so promptly that the news of the death of the Pope coincides with the news of the election of the successor. The adversaries begin to lose courage.

> "The new Pope, putting the enemy to rout and overcoming every obstacle, guides the ship right up

to the two columns and comes to rest between them; he makes it fast with a light chain that hangs from the bow to an anchor of the column on which stands the Host; and with another light chain which hangs from the stern, he fastens it at the opposite end to another anchor hanging from the column on which stands the Immaculate Virgin.

"Then a great convulsion takes place. All the ships that until then had fought against the Pope's ship are scattered; they flee away, collide and break to pieces one against another. Some sink and try to sink others. Several small ships that had fought gallantly for the Pope race to be the first to bind themselves to those two columns.

"Many other ships, having retreated through fear of the battle, cautiously watch from far away; the wrecks of the broken ships having been scattered in the whirlpools of the sea, they in their turn sail in good earnest to those two columns, and, having reached them, they make themselves fast to the hooks hanging down from them and there they remain safe, together with the principal ship, on which is the Pope. Over the sea there reigns a great calm."

Bosco explained his dreams as, "The enemy ships are persecutions. The most serious trials for the Church are near at hand... Her enemies are represented by the ships that tried to sink the ship if they could. Only two means are left to save her amidst so much confusion: Devotion to Mary Most Holy and frequent Communion, making use of every means and doing our best to practice them and having them practiced everywhere and by everybody."

Some people say that John Paul II was the Pope who was "gravely wounded," and his second attack was Parkinson's Disease, which eventually killed him.

In the later part of the dream, some people read Freemasonry into the story, especially the part about the two columns.

The dream can have many interpretations. It's complex enough that neither of us is eager to say whether it refers to current Papal issues, or if it clearly relates to the Saint Malachy predictions.

But, whatever else it is, and no matter what it really means, it's a very precise dream with enough detail and action to be interesting.

Did the Garabandal messages predict the last Pope?

The Garabandal visions -- sometimes described as apparitions -- appeared from 1961 to 1965 and seemed to be Saint Michael the Archangel and the Blessed Virgin Mary, referred to as "Our Lady of Mount Carmel of Garabandal", because she looked so much like Our Lady of Mount Carmel.

These appearances took place at San Sebastián de Garabandal in the Peña Sagra mountains in Spain. Massive crowds gathered to witness them, and it's said that these visions -- seen by many -- occurred at least a thousand times over five years. Many witnesses say that miraculous phenomena occurred. Some of it was captured in photographs and in movies.

The women receiving the visions were Mari Loli Mazón (May 1, 1949 – April 20, 2009), Jacinta González (born April 27, 1949), Mari Cruz González (born June 21, 1950) and Conchita González (born February 7, 1949).

The four girls said there were two main messages. The first message was:

> "*We must make many sacrifices, perform much penance, and visit the Blessed Sacrament frequently. But first, we must lead good lives. If we do not, a chastisement will befall us. The cup is already filling up, and if we do not change, a very great chastisement will come upon us.*"

The second was much longer. It was delivered in 1965, and only received by Conchita Gonzalez. The Blessed Mother said the following, through St. Michael:

"As my Message of the 18th of October has not been complied with, and as it has not been made known to the world, I am telling you that this is the last one.

"Previously, the Cup was filling; now, it is brimming over. Many priests are following the road to perdition, and with them they are taking many more souls. Ever less importance is being given to the Holy Eucharist.

"We should turn the wrath of God away from us by our own efforts. If you ask His forgiveness with a sincere heart. He will pardon you.

"I, your Mother, through the intercession of St. Michael the Archangel, wish to tell you that you should make amends.

"You are now being given the last warnings. I love you very much, and I do not want your condemnation. Ask Us sincerely and We shall grant your plea. You must make more sacrifices. Reflect on the Passion of Jesus."

At the time, the Catholic Church determined that the visions were *non constat*. That is, they couldn't be confirmed as anything supernatural.

In 1970, Cardinal Seper, Prefect of the Congregation for the Sacred Doctrine of the Faith, made the church's position even more clear. In a letter, he said, "... the Holy See has never approved even indirectly the Garabandal movement... it has never encouraged or blessed Garabandal promoters or centers."

No matter how you regard the Garabandal visions, none of this predicts anything about the Pope.

One comment has been repeated as proof that the Garabandal visions were a hoax. However, the information was not delivered at the Garabandal site, but by Conchita upon hearing that Pope John XXIII had died. According to the stories, she said, "*Seguramente... Pues, ya no quedan mas que tres!*" (Surely, now there will be no more than three Popes!")

Popes Paul VI, John Paul I, John Paul II, and Benedict XVI have followed. So, Conchita's comment -- not necessarily a prediction or a message from Divinity -- was not true.

Have any *Popes* predicted the last Pope?

A variety of stories seem to reference the end times and circumstances related to the Pope. Some have more credibility than others. There are far too many to document.

However, one of the most startling is a story attributed to a 1909 General Chapter of the Franciscans audience with the Pope. According to the story, Pius X went into a brief trance. When he returned to full consciousness, he said:

> "What I have seen was terrible... Will it be myself? Will it be my successor? What is certain is that the Pope will quit Rome, and in fleeing from the Vatican he will have to walk over the dead bodies of his priests. Do not tell anyone while I am alive."

In other versions of that story, Pius says something that suggests the last Pope will be another *Pius*.

Yet another curious story describes a conversation overheard (or envisioned) on 13 October 1884 by Pope Leo XIII. Supposedly, that conversation was described as:

> The guttural voice, the voice of Satan in his pride, boasted to Our Lord: "I can destroy your Church."
>
> The gentle voice of Our Lord: "You can? Then go ahead and do so."
>
> Satan: "To do so, I need more time and more power." Our Lord: "How much time? How much power?
>
> Satan: "75 to 100 years, and a greater power over those who will give themselves over to my service."
>
> Our Lord: "You have the time, you will have the power. Do with them what you will."

After hearing that, Pope Leo XIII penned his Prayer to St. Michael, to protect us from Satan. The Pope ordered it to be said at the conclusion of every low Mass. (The "low Mass" was said by a priest, alone, and with no music. This practice was discontinued after Vatican II.)

In 1994, Pope John Paul II urged the faithful to continue to say the prayer, daily. (See "Prayers to Saint Michael" in the Appendix section at the back of this book.)

8. Nostradamus and the Last Pope

Many people want to believe that Nostradamus predicted the last Pope. After all, Nostradamus spoke about so many modern issues.

The quatrain most often quoted is in Century 5. It could indicate Pope Benedict XVI *or* Pope Francis.

Nostradamus 5/49

Century 5, Quatrain 49

> *Nul de l'Espaigne mais de l'antique France,*
> *Ne sera esleu pour le tremblant nacelle,*
> *A l'ennemy sera faicte fiance,*
> *Qui dans son regne sera peste cruelle.*

Popular English translation:

> *Not from Spain but from ancient France,*
> *Will be elected for the trembling bark,*
> *He will make a promise to the enemy,*
> *Who will cause great plague during his reign.*

Maybe the "bark" is also a pun. A *barque* — the ship of Peter — refers to the Holy Roman Church.

A "barque" is a ship with at least three masts (the Holy Trinity?). The Roman Catholic Church has regularly been referred to as a *boat* or *ship*. That's a New Testament idea. The church works as a "fisher of men."

The "trembling" indicated Pope John Paul II, who suffered from Parkinson's Disease.

Benedict XVI was the next elected Pope. Did he make a "promise to the enemy"? Did that launch a "great plague" during his reign... perhaps one that we don't know about, yet?

Sexual misconduct of past Catholic priests has been a "plague" within the church.. Did Benedict, early in his tenure as Pope, make a promise of silence if the priests would voluntarily retire to a monastery, or something like that?

Maybe the answer is far deeper, embedded in the strife and conflicts we've seen in global headlines. A secret agreement may yet be exposed.

Resigning as Pope is extraordinary. Rumors are inevitable, and some may turn out to be true.

No matter *what* the answer, one problem with using that quatrain for "last Pope" predictions is that it's in Century 5. Century 10, Quatrain 72, says: "L'an mil neuf cens nonante neuf sept mois," or "In 1999, in the seventh (or September?) month..."

That makes a Century 5 prediction unlikely — *but not impossible* — for the last Pope. The verses would have to be *far* out of sequence.

Maybe Nostradamus went out of his way to be cryptic.

Lee McCann gave evidence of this in his 1941 analysis of the quatrains, *Nostradamus, the Man Who Saw Through Time*. However, critics claim that McCann and others are selecting quatrains that suit their ends. They say McCann, et al, *contrive* to make Nostradamus seem prophetic.

Quatrain order and 9/11

Did Nostradamus predict 9/11 in quatrain 1/87? If so, it's proof that the quatrains aren't sequential.

Original French:

> "Ennosigée feu du centre de terre / Fera trembler autour de Cité neufue / Deux grands rochers long temps ferôt la guerre / Puis Arethusa rougira nouueau Fleuue."

One of the *sensational* translations:

> "Enormous-promontories on fire in the center of the mainland / Will cause trembling in the towers of the City of New York / Two great rock-monoliths continuously will be attacked / This is when air-vessels will turn-around to a new course."

To force that translation, the word Arethusa (Greek water nymph) became are-thusa, supposedly meaning air-vessels.

The *actual* translation:

> "Volcanic fire from the center of the earth / will
> cause trembling around the new city / Two great
> rocks will make war for a long time / Then Arethusa
> will turn red a new river."

Another Nostradamus quatrain might point to 9/11. It's
from Century 12, quatrain 52:

> "Two bodies, one head, fields divided in two / And
> then to reply to four unheard ones / Little ones for
> great ones, clear evil for them / Lightning at the
> tower of Aiguesmortes, worse for 'Eussouis'."

Did that predict the 9/11 World Trade Center disaster?

Two buildings, one site divided in two by a plaza, and
headlines involving four flights. "Aiguesmortes" as *auges
mortes* suggests a death with sharp pain. Further,
Nostradamus expert J. B. Hare pointed out that —
phonetically — "Eussouis" *could* be a garbled attempt at
"USA."

Nostradamus interpreter Daniel Fortin disagrees. Line
three in the original French quatrain says, "Petis pour
Grands. à Pertuis mal pour eux." Pertuis isn't necessarily
"evil." It's a town in Provence, France.

The French verse mentioned *Tour D'Aigues,* not
Aiguesmortes. Tour D'Aigues is about 6 km north of
Pertuis. In Fortin's opinion, the 12/52 quatrain hasn't
occurred yet. It's an event in Province, France.

Each side presents a good argument. We can't use 9/11 to
prove that the quatrains are out of order.

On the other hand, *Nostradamus* gave us hints.

Nostradamus' own explanation

Though Nostradamus' predictions are organized by
"centuries," that's usually accepted as 100 ("cent" meaning
100, in French) predictions, *not years.*

As Nostradamus said, "I have composed books of

prophecies, containing **each one hundred astronomic quatrains of forecasts**, which I have tried to polish through obscurely, and which are perpetual vaticinations, from now to the year 3797." (emphasis added)

There are *12* "centuries" in Nostradamus' work. On the calendar, there are *22* centuries between the 16th and 38th centuries. (Nostradamus said that his predictions covered the years from his own time to the year 3797.)

So, we know the "centuries" won't match the calendar.

Despite that, are the predictions (or quatrains) *sequential?*

In Michael Nostradamus' own preface to his predictions, he says, "...for the most part of future time... kingdoms, sects, and religions will pass through stages so very contrary, and, as regards the present time, diametrically opposed..."

He might have been hinting that the "stages" (or quatrains) would be literally "contrary" or "diametrically opposed" to his present-time predictions.

In other words, his prophecies may have been rearranged, deliberately.

He said that his writing would "declare in dark and abstruse sayings" ("abstruse" means written in a hidden manner).

Likewise, in his letter to King Henry II, Nostradamus said again, "the bulk of the prophetic quatrains are so rude, that there is no making way through them, nor is there any interpreter of them."

He also said, "Wherefore the independent causes being independently produced, or not produced, the presage partially happens, where it was predicted."

Taken *literally,* that suggests the quatrains stand alone, independent of one another, and the location ("where") may be more literal than the time sequence.

Then, he said, "I have more fully and at large set forth in *my other Prophecies,* which are drawn out at length... (in these I) designate the localities, times, and terms prefixed, that all men who come after may see, recognizing the circumstances that come about by infallible indications." (emphasis added)

Sadly, those "other Prophecies" were lost. Experts say those were in prose, not quatrains.

Our question is: Did that describe the quatrains, as well? Are the "times" indicated literally, by sequence? Or, did he mean that the locations and *signs of the times* were infallible indications?

We're not sure.

You, the reader, must decide.

How quatrain 5/49 fits Pope Francis

Some Nostradamus experts say that this quatrain *definitely* indicated Pope Francis.

Here's that quatrain again:

Not from Spain but from ancient France / Will be elected for the trembling bark / He will make a promise to the enemy / Who will cause great plague during his reign.

- Though Pope Francis was born in a country where Spanish is the dominant language, the Pope is not Spanish.

- The reference to "ancient France" might also point to Pope Francis. His name, Francis, has several meanings, include "French-ish."

Will Pope Francis makes a promise to the enemy, that later causes great troubles? Could it be a *literal* plague? For the latter, we'd expect a leak of research materials involving viruses or bacteria, or — even worse — germ warfare or chemical weapons.

Some Petrus Romanus experts claim the plague is connected to the Vatican's secret agreements with aliens who need a new world for their species to continue. Variations of that theory involves clearing out much of Africa as the new homeland of the alien race.

Supporters point to the TV series, The Event. They specifically recommend the "Cut Off the Head" episode.

We'll admit that's a compelling coincidence. We also think it's far-fetched. We're looking for something more realistic.

Nostradamus 5/25 and the Popes

Nostradamus didn't make easy to interpret his predictions. Some people point to Century 5, Quatrain 25, for the reign of Petrus Romanus:

> *Le prince Arabe Mars, Sol, Venus, Lyon*
> *Regne d'Eglise par mer succombera:*
> *Deuers la Perse bien pres d'vn million,*
> *Bisance, Egypte ver. serp. inuadera.*

Here's the classic English translation:

> The Arab Prince Mars, Sun, Venus, Leo,
> The rule of the Church will succumb by sea:
> Towards Persia very nearly a million men,
> The true serpent will invade Byzantium and Egypt.

Here's the same quatrain, translated using more modern geography and political references:

> Muslims, wars, the Day of the Lord, the Harlot, the Lioness Beast
> The reign of the Church from the sea shall be succumbed
> Toward Iran one shall see nearly one million troops
> Turkey, Egypt, evils shall the true serpent* invade.

*The "serpent" has been interpreted in a variety of ways, from "evils" in general to the Antichrist and his servants, to the Illuminati, to NATO forces, and so on. It all depends on your ideology.

Nevertheless, though we're not sure how to interpret the "*Le prince Arabe Mars, Sol, Venus, Lyon*" passage, there's an interesting note, similar to punctuation issues in the 112th prediction of the Saint Malachy prophecy: Different people seem to place commas in various places in the first line of Nostradamus 5/25.

Le prince Arabe, Mars, Sol separates the Arab prince from Mars, Sol, and so on.

Le prince Arabe Mars, Sol suggests that the Arab prince is like Mars, the god of war.

Le prince Arabe Mars Sol, Venus, Lyon offers a variety of interpretations, including an Arab prince of war who shines like the sun (literally or figuratively).

Century 5 may also include other recent references. For example, in Century 5, Quatrain 92, it says:

> *Apres le siege tenu dixscept ans,*
> *Cinq changeront en tel reuolu terme:*
> *Puis sera l'vn esleu de mesme temps,*
> *Qui des Romains ne sera trop conforme.*

> After the [Holy] See has been held seventeen years,
> Five will change within the same period of time:
> Then one will be elected at the same time,
> One who will not be too conformable to the Romans.

Pius XI reigned for 17 years. He was followed by Pius XII (1939-58), John XXIII (1958-63), Paul VI (1963-78), John Paul I (1978), and John Paul II (1978 – 2005).

Might the Pope who followed them — Benedict XVI — and "the same time" refer to *two* elected Popes... one who resigned (Benedict) and one who accepted the seat at the Vatican (Francis)?

We're not sure which of them might be the one who's not "too conformable" (bendable, malleable, or easily swayed) in terms of traditional Vatican and church opinions.

If Nostradamus' predictions aren't *always* sequential, maybe Nostradamus 5/49 *also* references Pope Benedict XVI.

The family tree of Cardinal Joseph Aloisius Ratzinger (Pope Benedict XVI)

In Nostradamus 5/49, there is a reference to someone "not

from Spain but ancient France."

Many people say that it means the bloodline of the last (111th) Pope in St. Malachy's prophecy. Legend says that the last *real* Pope would be from the bloodline of ancient French kings.

Unfortunately, we can't connect Benedict XVI with the ancient French or Merovingian kings. Here's what we *do* know. Maybe you can extend the family tree and connect it with France.

Joseph Alois Ratzinger was born at 4:15 AM on 16 April 1927 in his family's home at 11 Schulstrasse in Marktl (or *Marktl am Inn*), Bavaria, Germany. He was baptized at 8:30 AM that same day. The day was Holy Saturday, and — as the Pope's brother, Georg recalls — it was an unusually snowy month.

Marktl is a small town on the river Inn, with less than 3,000 residents covering 10 square miles. It's full name, Marktl am Inn, means "little market on the river Inn."

A couple of historical notes that may be useful, later: Marktl's first church was the Church of Saint Oswald, built in 1297. In 1701, lightning struck the church and resulted in the destruction of the entire market.

Marktl, connected to the *Autobahn A 94,* and Passau are about 68 km apart from each other. That's less than an hour's drive, by car.

Passau is the nearest community where births such as Cardinal Ratzinger's were *registered*. Passau is known as the "city of three rivers." That reference — as well as the nickname and history of Marktl — may help as we try to unravel the Papal predictions of people such as Saint Malachy and Nostradamus.

Joseph A. Ratzinger's parents were Joseph Ratzinger (6 Mar 1877 – 25 Aug 1959, Germany) and Maria Peintner (7 Jan 1884 – 16 Dec 1963, Germany). They were married on 11 Sep 1920.

Joseph Ratzinger (1877 – 1959), a police officer, was the

son of John Ratzinger (born ca. 1850).

Maria Peintner's ancestry is unknown, but may have come from the area of South Tyrol (Austria) . More likely, her family is from Tyrolsberg, Neumarkt in der Oberpfalz, Bavaria, Germany. Her brothers may have included Georg Peintner, Dinzo Peintner and Eduard Peintner, who served in World War I.

Tip for researchers: In many European families, the oldest son is usually named after his *paternal* grandfather. The second son is often named after his *maternal* grandfather. The third son is usually named after his father (unless the name is already in use) or another family member or close family friend.

The family tree of Pope Francis

We haven't had time to delve deeply into Pope Francis' family tree to see if it matches the French connection in Nostradamus' prediction.

One hurdle is the Pope's Italian ancestry. Italian family history isn't always as *thoroughly* documented as the Germany ancestry of Cardinal Ratzinger (Pope Benedict XVI).

Italian church records are usually required, and they aren't as accessible — or as easy to understand — as many records we work with.

However, Pope Francis' Bergoglio ancestry is from around Turin. With such northern roots, *some* French ancestry is probably in the mix. Of course, that's speculation based on geography. Nothing is certain, yet.

The Pope's mother, Regina María Sivori, was born in Argentina but her family was also from an area about 250 miles north of Rome, Italy. Records are somewhat confusing, even more than Italian records. In both cases, Catholic Church records are part of the research.

We don't want to rush this and make a mistake. *Early* searches suggest that her immigrant ancestor was Juan Jose Sivori (1884 – ?), who moved to Buenos Aires in

January 1917, via London, England. (We may revise that later, when we have more records to work with.)

Predictions say the Pope will flee Rome by boat. Then, he'll travel to Germany. Finally, he'll establish a new base at the ancient French Papal site of Avignon.

That *could* fit Pope Francis, especially if he were traveling back to an ancestral French homeland.

Nostradamus 10/72, revisited

Century 10, quatrain 72 is remarkable because it provides a specific year, 1999.

> *L'an mil neuf cens nonante neuf sept mois,*
> *Du ciel viendra un gran Roy effrayeur.*
> *Resusciter le grand Roy d'Angolmois.*
> *Avant apres Mars regner par bon heur.*

Here's one translation:

> In the year 1999 and seven months,
> From the Heavens will come a great King of Terror.
> The great king of Angolmois will be resuscitated (brought back to life),
> Before and after March reigns by early hour.

Some have gone to great lengths to make this fit the transfer of power from Pope Benedict XVI to Pope Francis. They claim:

- 1999 plus seven months is the year 2000.
- The "King of Terror" is the Death card in the Tarot, indicating the number 13. So, that leads to the year 2013.
- The great king of Anolmois was Francis I.
- The "early hour" was Benedict XVI's resignation before the start of March.

We'd say that's a preposterous stretch... *but is it?* That interpretation is interesting.

Nostradamus on End Times

In Nostradamus' letter to his son, he said:

"I find the world before the universal conflagration, such deluges and deep submersion, that ***there will remain scarcely any land not covered with water***, and that for so long a period, that everything will perish except Ethnographies and Topographies.

"Further, after and before these inundations, in many districts the rains will have been so slight, and there will fall from heaven such an abundance of fire and incandescent stones, that scarcely anything will remain unconsumed, and ***this will occur a short time before the last conflagration***." (emphasis added)

9. Numerology and the Last Pope

Is Pope Francis the last Pope? Is he even a *real* Pope? Is he *Petrus Romanus?* That's been the subject of heated debate since his March 2013 election.

After Pope Francis was announced, several people raised concerns. Their evidence is worth considering.

As we mentioned earlier, Pope Francis chose a very *odd* phrase as he described his election. He said "fine del mondo," or "the end of the world."

That's been interpreted as a joke, but — in light of *Petrus Romanus* predictions — it's a strange phrase to use.

That's not *all* that startled St. Malachy believers during this transfer of power to the new Pope.

Unlike his predecessors, Pope Francis *didn't add a number to his name.* If you look at recent Papal elections to verify the naming traditions, you'll see that Pope John Paul I was — from the very beginning — Pope John Paul I.

This suggests that Pope Francis expects no Pope Francis II to follow. In fact, if he has insights that we don't, he may expect *no* Popes to follow him.

(We expect the Vatican to amend Pope Francis' name. Already, the press has begun to call him Pope Francis I, but the initial slip did *not* escape attention.)

Then, Pope Francis announced that his name reflected St. Francis of Assisi.

St. Francis of Assisi's real name was Francesco di *Pietro* de Bernardone. So, there's the "Peter" connection to Petrus Romanus.

While the media are declaring Pope Francis an Argentinian, his ancestry is Italian. The Pope's birth name was *Jorge Mario Bergoglio.* His father was an Italian immigrant. The Bergoglio family is traditionally from the Turin area... famous for the Shroud of Turn. Pope Francis' mother's family was also from Italy, about 250 miles north of Rome.

So, Pope Francis' roots fit the "Romanus" requirements of being Italian.

Maybe Pope Francis *is* Petrus Romanus. Time will tell.

Meanwhile, *Time* magazine declared Pope Francis the "New World Pope." Pope Francis *does* have a "New World" association with the Americas. But... was *Time* magazine sending a message about the New World Order?

We may be grasping at straws. Maybe *Petrus Romanus* was at the helm of the church *before* Pope Francis.

We need look no further than Cardinal Bertone.

Cardinal Bertone

Cardinal Tarcisio *Pietro* Evasio Bertone almost evaded our attention. After all, he's been such a bumbling manager of PR for the Vatican, who could suspect him of *anything* requiring cleverness? Now, we wonder if he's as devious and deceptive as Professor Quirrell in the *Harry Potter* novels.

His name is *Peter*. He's from *Romano* Cavanese, and he sat as titular head of the Vatican immediately after Pope Benedict XVI stepped down, before the election of Pope Francis. Those are three *strong* points matching the Petrus Romanus prediction.

If Bertone filled the role of Petrus Romanus... *who is Pope Francis?*

We're not sure. We're watching as this story unfolds.

Other predictions

Let's not overlook *other* evidence. It might reveal where we are in terms of St. Malachy's *Petrus Romanus* sequence.

As you've seen, Nostradamus' predictions might indicate the era of the last Pope. However, *numbers* may be more helpful.

We feel this is *supporting* evidence. It's not enough to

stand on its own. At the very least, it's *interesting*.

Pope Benedict XVI and numerology

Using the Pope's childhood name, Joseph Alois Ratzinger, we see the following numerological results:

His main number is 4. That indicates someone whose life is best dedicated in service to others. A person with the number 4 prefers order, but also struggles against the very structure that brings him comfort. It is through that struggle, and finding balance, that he achieves personal growth and development.

His soul number is 6, which indicates someone with an extraordinary commitment to others, and an unusual level of energy to do so. However, he runs the risk of burnout, and must learn to say no to some requests. Otherwise, the drain on his energy will require rest or retirement, at least for awhile.

His inner number — the one associated with his dreams and spiritual site — is 7. (His chosen Papal name, Benedict, is also a 7. And, as Benedict XVI, his title number — 16 — adds up to 7, as well.) As a 7, he's extraordinarily lucky. He'll also seek shelter from worldly distractions. A 7 discovers meaning in serving others as a teacher or spiritual leader. For those inclined to privacy and introspection, a monastic life is preferred. A 7 may also be a mystic.

Using the name of Benedict XVI as letters, ignoring the numerical intent of "XVI," we see that "benedict xvi" has a main number of 9. In many cultures, the number 9 (nine) is the final step before something concludes. It's the last single-digit number. It rolls over to 1 (back to the beginning) or 10 (a new, expanded beginning).

Malachy's "last Pope," numerology, and logoprosodic analysis

Logoprosodic analysis is the study of works — usually writing — based on numerical values. Logotechnique presents the idea that the Bible (and perhaps other inspired and Scriptural works) have a numeric structure.

It's complicated. Take our word for it.

But, if this is your kind of challenge, the following are numbers that may be useful.

According to Gunnar Tomasson in the <u>Bibal Study Group</u> (Yahoo! Groups), the following numbers relate to the 112th prophecy:

> In persecutione extrema S.R.E. = 13831
>
> sedebit Petrus Romanus, = 12051
>
> qui pascet oues in multis tribulationibus: = 22136
>
> quibus transactis ciuitas septicollis diruetur, = 26227
>
> & Iudex tremêdus iudicabit populum suum. Finis. = 22573 = 96818

Of course, now we're back to the issue of *where the lines break in the 112th prediction.* In some calculations, the break can make a significant difference in the number patterns and numerological interpretation.

As an example, let's return to an easier and more straightforward numerical analysis.

Simple numerology and the 112th Pope

Using *simple* numerology, here's what we see in connection with the 112th prediction by Malachy:

In persecutione extrema S.R.E = 4 (The same as Pope Benedict XVI's name when he was a cardinal.)

In persecutione extrema S.R.E. sedebit = 5

In psecutione extrema S.R.E.sedebit (as spelled in the 1595 printing) = 9

Once again, this last, most accurate numerical analysis points to 9. It's the number of a *final step before a conclusion,* followed by a new beginning. (See our discussion of *In persecutione extrema S.R.E. sedebit —* "In extreme persecution the Holy Roman Church *sits.*" That's explained in our chapter, "What Was St. Malachy's Prophecy?")

This topic that could fill an entire book. Numerology can be a starting point for more research.

Jonathan Edwards – confirming what the numbers indicate?

The "old world, new world" concept — represented by the number 9 and what follows it — is echoed in much of the work by Jonathan Edwards (1703 – 1758). In his epic work, *The History of Redemption,* Edwards says (emphasis added):

"**Before, things were in a kind of preparatory state, but now they are in a finishing state**: it is the winding up of things which is all this while accomplishing. Heaven and earth began to shake in order to a dissolution, according to the prophecy of Haggai, before Christ came, that so only 'those things that cannot be shaken may remain,' Heb. xii. 27 ; that is, that those things which are to come to an end, may come to an end, and that only those things may remain, which are to remain eternally.

"...So, in the first place, the carnal ordinances of the Jewish worship came to an end, to make way for the establishment of that spiritual worship, the worship of the heart, which is to endure to eternity; "Jesus saith unto the woman, Believe me, the hour cometh, when ye shall neither in this mountain, nor yet at Jerusalem, worship the Father.—But the hour cometh, and now is, when the true worshippers shall worship the Father in spirit and in truth ; for the Father seeketh such to worship him," *John iv. 21. 23.* This is one instance of **the temporary world's coming to an end, and the eternal world's beginning.**

"Another instance is, that the outward temple, and the city of Jerusalem, came to an end, to give place to the setting up of the spiritual temple and the city, which are to endure for ever; which is also another instance of removing those things which are ready to vanish away, that those things which cannot be shaken may remain. Again, the old heathen empire comes to an end, to make way for the everlasting empire of Christ.

"**Upon the fall of antichrist, an end will be put to**

Satan's visible kingdom on earth, to establish Christ's eternal kingdom; 'And the kingdom and dominion, and the greatness of the kingdom under the whole heaven, shall be given to the people of the saints of the most High, whose kingdom is an everlasting kingdom, and all domi nions shall serve and obey him,' *Dan. vii. 27.* which is another instance of the ending of the temporary world, and the beginning of the eternal one.

"And then, lastly, the very frame of this corruptible world shall come to an end, to make way for the church to dwell in another dwelling place, which shall last to eternity.

"Because the world is thus coming to an end by various steps and degrees, the apostle perhaps uses this expression, that not the end, but the ends of the world are come on us; as though the world has several endings one after another.

"...That state of things which is attained in the events of this period is called 'a new heaven and a new earth;' '**For behold, I create new heavens and a new earth: and the former shall not be remembered, nor come into mind.** But be ye glad and rejoice for ever in that which I create; for behold, I create Jerusalem a rejoicing, and her people a joy,' *Isa. lxv. 17,18.* And *ch. lxvi. 22.* '**For as the new heavens and new earth which I will make, shall remain before me, saith the Lord, so shall your seed and your name remain.**' See also *ch. li. 16.*"

 For those who are prepared, we think Edwards' views provide comfort rather than fear, when we think of end times. It's another of those silver linings we rely on — along with some humor — to keep this research from becoming too grim.

10. Jesus' Mount of Olives Prophecy, Daniel's Visions

We think it's appropriate in this book for Jesus to have the last word on the topic of the end times. All of these quotations are from the King James Version (KJV) of the Bible.

The Book of Matthew - Chapter 24

1 And Jesus went out, and departed from the temple: and his disciples came to him for to shew him the buildings of the temple.

2 **And Jesus said unto them, See ye not all these things? verily I say unto you, There shall not be left here one stone upon another, that shall not be thrown down.**

3 **And as he sat upon the mount of Olives, the disciples came unto him privately, saying, Tell us, when shall these things be? and what shall be the sign of thy coming, and of the end of the world?**

4 **And Jesus answered and said unto them, Take heed that no man deceive you.**

5 **For many shall come in my name, saying, I am Christ; and shall deceive many.**

6 **And ye shall hear of wars and rumours of wars: see that ye be not troubled: for all these things must come to pass, but the end is not yet.**

7 **For nation shall rise against nation, and kingdom against kingdom: and there shall be famines, and pestilences, and earthquakes, in divers places.**

8 **All these are the beginning of sorrows.**

9 Then shall they deliver you up to be afflicted, and shall kill you: and ye shall be hated of all nations for my name's sake.

10 And then shall many be offended, and shall betray one another, and shall hate one another.

11 **And many false prophets shall rise, and shall deceive many.**

12 And because iniquity shall abound, the love of many shall wax cold.

13 But he that shall endure unto the end, the same shall be saved.

14 **And this gospel of the kingdom shall be preached in all the world for a witness unto all nations; and then shall the end come.**

15 **When ye therefore shall see the abomination of desolation, spoken of by Daniel the prophet, stand in the holy place, (whoso readeth, let him understand:)**

> *Daniel 8*
>
> *23 And in the latter time of their kingdom, when the transgressors are come to the full, a king of fierce countenance, and understanding dark sentences, shall stand up.*
>
> *24 And his power shall be mighty, but not by his own power: and he shall destroy wonderfully, and shall prosper, and practise, and shall destroy the mighty and the holy people.*
>
> *25 And through his policy also he shall cause craft to prosper in his hand; and he shall magnify himself in his heart, and by peace shall destroy many: he shall also stand up against the Prince of princes; but he shall be broken without hand.*
>
> *26 And the vision of the evening and the morning which was told is true: wherefore shut thou up the vision; for it shall be for many days.*
>
> *Daniel 9:26 And after threescore and two weeks shall Messiah be cut off, but not for himself: and the people of the prince that shall come shall*

destroy the city and the sanctuary; and the end thereof shall be with a flood, and unto the end of the war desolations are determined.

Daniel 12

And at that time shall Michael stand up, the great prince which standeth for the children of thy people: and there shall be a time of trouble, such as never was since there was a nation even to that same time: and at that time thy people shall be delivered, every one that shall be found written in the book.

2 And many of them that sleep in the dust of the earth shall awake, some to everlasting life, and some to shame and everlasting contempt.

3 And they that be wise shall shine as the brightness of the firmament; and they that turn many to righteousness as the stars for ever and ever.

4 But thou, O Daniel, shut up the words, and seal the book, even to the time of the end: many shall run to and fro, and knowledge shall be increased.

5 Then I Daniel looked, and, behold, there stood other two, the one on this side of the bank of the river, and the other on that side of the bank of the river.

6 And one said to the man clothed in linen, which was upon the waters of the river, How long shall it be to the end of these wonders?

7 And I heard the man clothed in linen, which was upon the waters of the river, when he held up his right hand and his left hand unto heaven, and sware by him that liveth for ever that it shall be for a time, times, and an half; and when he shall have accomplished to scatter the power of the holy people, all these things shall be finished.

⁸ And I heard, but I understood not: then said I, O my Lord, what shall be the end of these things?

⁹ And he said, Go thy way, Daniel: for the words are closed up and sealed till the time of the end.

¹⁰ Many shall be purified, and made white, and tried; but the wicked shall do wickedly: and none of the wicked shall understand; but the wise shall understand.

¹¹ And from the time that the daily sacrifice shall be taken away, and the abomination that maketh desolate set up, there shall be a thousand two hundred and ninety days.

¹² Blessed is he that waiteth, and cometh to the thousand three hundred and five and thirty days.

¹³ But go thou thy way till the end be: for thou shalt rest, and stand in thy lot at the end of the days.

16 **Then let them which be in Judaea flee into the mountains:**

17 **Let him which is on the housetop not come down to take any thing out of his house:**

18 **Neither let him which is in the field return back to take his clothes.**

19 And woe unto them that are with child, and to them that give suck in those days!

20 But pray ye that your flight be not in the winter, neither on the sabbath day:

21 **For then shall be great tribulation, such as was not since the beginning of the world to this time, no, nor ever shall be.**

22 **And except those days should be shortened, there should no flesh be saved: but for the elect's sake those days shall be shortened.**

23 **Then if any man shall say unto you, Lo, here is**

Christ, or there; believe it not.

24 For there shall arise false Christs, and false prophets, and shall shew great signs and wonders; insomuch that, if it were possible, they shall deceive the very elect.

...

29 Immediately after the tribulation of those days shall the sun be darkened, and the moon shall not give her light, and the stars shall fall from heaven, and the powers of the heavens shall be shaken:

30 And then shall appear the sign of the Son of man in heaven: and then shall all the tribes of the earth mourn, and they shall see the Son of man coming in the clouds of heaven with power and great glory.

31 And he shall send his angels with a great sound of a trumpet, and they shall gather together his elect from the four winds, from one end of heaven to the other.

32 Now learn a parable of the fig tree; When his branch is yet tender, and putteth forth leaves, ye know that summer is nigh:

33 So likewise ye, when ye shall see all these things, know that it is near, even at the doors.

...

40 Then shall two be in the field; the one shall be taken, and the other left.

41 Two women shall be grinding at the mill; the one shall be taken, and the other left.

42 Watch therefore: for ye know not what hour your Lord doth come.

43 But know this, that if the goodman of the house had known in what watch the thief would come, he would have watched, and would not have suffered his house to be broken up.

44 Therefore be ye also ready: for in such an hour as ye think not the Son of man cometh.

Also see **1 Thessalonians 4**

16 For the Lord himself shall descend from heaven with a shout, with the voice of the archangel, and with the trump of God: and the dead in Christ shall rise first:

17 Then we which are alive and remain shall be caught up together with them in the clouds, to meet the Lord in the air: and so shall we ever be with the Lord.

Appendixes

What Other Popes Resigned?

Pope Benedict XVI wasn't the *first* Pope to resign, but his was certainly the most surprising resignation, and one of the most heart-wrenching for many Catholics.

The following Popes resigned in the past. They're arranged in reverse date order, with the most recent at the top.

1415 - Gregory XII

The last resignation of a Pope was on July 4th, 1415 when Pope Gregory XII (Angelo Correr) concluded his tenure, having reigned since 1406. His resignation followed considerable turmoil and division within the Roman Catholic Church, as Rome and Avignon (and sometimes Pisa) declared their popes the *only* official ones. Over several turbulent years, the two popes argued and even excommunicated each other.

1415 was a critical year in church history, as the Council of Constance religious reformers John Wycliffe and Jan Hus were condemned as heretics.

> John Wycliffe -- born in 1320 in Yorkshire, England -- was among those who promoted the translation of the Bible, and is generally credited with the first *complete* Bible translation into English. (Portions had been translated starting as early as the seventh century.)

> Jan Hus -- a Czech priest born around 1369 in Southern Bohemia -- openly based many of his ideas on Wycliffe's "heretical" beliefs. Hus (also known as John Huss) is regarded as one of the key forerunners to the Protestant movement of Martin Luther, which followed in the 16th century.

> In 1415 in Germany, the Council of Constance condemned Hus. On July 6th -- two days after

Pope Gregory XII resigned -- when Hus was brought to the Cathedral at Konstanz, Hus refused to recant. He was led from the cathedral, undressed, a tall paper hat put on his head (saying "Haeresiarcha," or "leader of heretics") and burned at the stake. His ashes were thrown into the Rhine river.

The council also ordered the burning of all Wycliffe's books and exhumation of his body. It, too, was burned and the ashes cast into the River Swift, a tributary of the River Avon that flows through Lutterworth (Leicestershire) and Warwickshire, England.

Today, July 6th is a public holiday in the Czeck Republic, and known as *Jan Hus Day*. His life and death are also commemorated by the Episcopal Church and the Evangelical Lutheran Church in America.

Jan Hus is also remembered as the man who -- during his heresy trial -- made statements about Pope Joan. According to many people, his statements about her were the only ones not refuted and condemned during the trial.

Wycliffe is remember at the end of December each year, by the Church of England and the Anglican Church of Canada, and at the end of October by the Episcopal Church. Despite the burning order -- and a subsequent death sentence for any unlicensed person holding a copy of the Scriptures in English -- 250 manuscripts of the Wycliffe Bible still exist.

St. Celestine V

Pope Celestine V resigned after just five months (5 July 1294 – 13 December 1294). According to stories, his election as Pope may have been hasty.

For two years after the death of Pope Nicholas IV, the cardinals still could not agree on a new Pope. To many, the church was drifting without a leader.

A well-known hermetic month, Pietro di Morrone, sent the cardinals a letter warning them that divine vengeance would fall upon them if they did not soon reach an agreement about a Pope.

After the letter was read aloud, Latino Malabranca, the aged dean of the College of Cardinals exclaimed, "In the name of the Father, the Son, and the Holy Ghost, I elect brother Pietro di Morrone." His fellow cardinals promptly agreed and voted for Pietro di Morrone, who reluctantly accepted and became Pope Celestine V.

He felt overwhelmed by the tasks necessary to lead the church, and resumed his hermetic life. In 1313, he was canonized as a saint. No other Pope has taken the name Celestine.

Gregory VI

Gregory VI was Pope for about a year (April/May 1045 – 20 December 1046) when he either abdicated or was deposed. He freely admitted to buying his way into the Papacy. Realizing that he couldn't escape being deposed, he resigned.

Benedict IX

Benedict IV was Pope *three times* between 1032 and 1048. Although a popular man, and the youngest Pope ever, at one point he sold the Papacy to his godfather, Gregory VI, and resigned.

Other Popes

The above list includes the only Popes who *clearly* resigned, though not all were completely voluntary.

Several other Popes *may* have resigned, but the documentation isn't strong enough to be sure:

- John XVIII (January 1004 – July 1009)
- Liberius (17 May 352 – 24 September 366)
- Marcellinus (30 June 296 – 1 April 304)
- Pope Pontian (21 July 230 – 28 September 235)

Complete Malachy Prophecy List

The following is a list* of Popes and antipopes (and a few who were close to being antipopes). This isn't a full list of every Catholic Pope, *ever*. It's only those that might correspond with the Malachy prophecy.

The antipopes do not have official sequential numbers; some have verses but others don't.

Also, the *Catholic Encyclopedia* lists Celestine II as the 166th Pope. Numbering systems vary. What's important for this study is the sequence on the *right* side, indicating which Malachy verse is referenced.

Pope's name and tenure / Malachy's sequence and motto.

167 Celstine II (1143-1144) / 1 Ex castro Tyberis. (From Tyber castle)
168 Lucius II (1144-1145) / 2 Inimicus expulsus. (Enemy expelled)
169 Blessed Eugene III (1145-1153) / 3 Ex magnitudine montis. (Out of the greatness of the mountain)
170 Anastasius IV (1153-1154) / 4 Abbas Suburranus. (Of the Suburra family)
171 Adrian IV (1154-1159) / 5 De rure albo. (From the white countryside)

Antipopes
Victor IV (1159-1164) / 6 Ex tetro carcere. (Of a loathsome prison)
Paschal III (1164-1168) / 7 Via trans-Tyberina. (Road across the Tyber)
Calistus III (1168-1178) / 8 De Pannonia Tusciae. (From Tusculan Hungary)
Innocent III (1179-1180) ... no Malachy reference, he lasted a little over three months before exile.
----

172 Alexander III (1159-1181) / 9   Ex ansere custode. (Out of the guardian goose)

173 Lucius III (1181-1185) / 10   Lux in ostio. (Light in the distance)

174 Urban III (1185-1187) / 11   Sus in cribo. (Pig in a sieve)

175 Gregory VIII (1187) / 12   Ensis Laurentii. (Sword of Lawrence)

176 Clement III (1187-1191) / 13   De schola exiet. (Will go out from school)

177 Celestine III (1191-1198) / 14   De rure bovensi. (Of cattle country)

178 Innocent III (1198-1216) / 15   Comes signatus. (Designated count)

179 Honorius III (1216-1227) / 16   Canonicus de latere. (Canon from the side)

180 Gregory IX (1227-1241) / 17   Avis Ostiensis. (Bird of Ostia)

181 Celestine IV (1241) / 18   Leo Sabinus. (Sabina lion)

182 Innocent IV (1243-1254) / 19   Comes Laurentius. (Count Lawrence)

183 Alexander IV (1254-1261) / 20   Signum Ostiense. (Sign of Ostia)

184 Urban IV (1261-1264) / 21   Hierusalem Campaniae. (Jerusalem of Champaign)

185 Clement IV (1265-1268) /22   Draco depressus. (Dragon pressed down)

186 Gregory X (1271-1276) / 23   Anguinus vir. (Snaky man)

187 Innocent V (1276) /24   Concionatur Gallus. (French preacher)

188 Adrian V (1276) /25   Bonus Comes. (Good Count)

189 John XXI (1276-1277) /26   Piscator Tuscus. (Tuscan fisherman)

190 Nicholas III (1277-1280) / 27   Rosa composita. (Composite rose)

191 Martin IV (1281-1285) / 28   Ex teloneo liliacei Martini. (From a tollhouse lilied, of Martin)

192 Honorius IV (1285-1287) / 29   Ex rosa leonina. (Out of the leonine rose)

193 Nicholas IV (1288-1292) /30   Picus inter escas. (Woodpecker between food)

194 St. Celestine V (1294) /31   Ex eremo celsus. (Raised from the desert)

195 Boniface VIII (1294-1303) / 32   Ex undarum benedictione. (From waves blessed)

196 Benedict XI (1303-1304) /33   Concionator patereus. (Preacher suffered, or from Patara)

197 Clement V (1305-1314) /34   De fessis Aquitanicis. (Of the fesses of Aquitaine)

198 John XXII (1316-1334) /35   De sutore osseo. (Of a bony cobbler)

Antipope
Nicholas V (1328-1330) /36   Corvus schismaticus. (Schismatic crow)

----

199 Benedict XII (1334-1342) /37   Frigidus Abbas. (Cold abbot)

200 Clement VI (1342-1352) / 38   De rosa Attrebatensi. (Of the rose of Arras)

201 Innocent VI (1352-1362) / 39   De montibus Pammachii. (Of the mountains of Pammachius)

202 Urban V (1362-1370) / 40   Gallus Vice-comes. (French viscount)

203 Gregory XI (1370-1378) /41   Novus de Virgine forti. (New man from strong virgin)

Antipopes
Clement VII (1378-1394) /42   De cruce Apostilica. (Of the apostolic cross)

Benedict XIII (1394-1423) /43   Luna Cosmedina. (Cosmedine moon)

Clement VIII (1423-1429) /44   Schisma Barcinonicum. (Schism of the Barcelonas)

Benedict XIV (1425-?) ... not included in Malachy's prophecies

----

204 Urban VI (1378-1389) / 45   De Inferno praegnanti. (Of a pregnant Hell)

205 Boniface IX (1389-1404) / 46   Cubus de mixtione. (Mixture of cubes or squares)

206 Innocent VII (1404-1406) /47   De meliore sydere. (Of

a better star)
207 Gregory XII (1406-1415) / 48   Nauta de ponte nigro.
(Sailor of a dark bridge)

Antipopes
Alexander V (1409-1410) /49   Flagellum Solis. (Whip of
the Sun)
John XIII (1410-1415) /50   Cervus Sirenae. (Stag of sirens)

----

208 Martin V (1417-1431) /51   Corona veli aurei. (Crown of
golden curtain)
209 Eugene IV (1431-1447) / 52   Lupa caelestina. (She-
wolf of the heavens)

Antipope
Felix V (1439-1449) / 53   Amator crucis. (Lover of the
cross)

----

210 Nicholas V (1447-1455) / 54   De modicitate lunae.
(Modesty, or humility, of Luna)
211 Callistus III (1455-1458) /55   Bos pascens. (Cattle
feeding)
212 Pius II (1458-1464) /56   De capra et Albergo. (Goat
and Albergo)
213 Paul II (1464-1471) /57   De cervo et Leone. (Of a stag
and lion)
214 Sixtus IV (1471-1484) /58   Piscator Minorita.
(Minority, or Minorite, fisherman)
215 Innocent VIII (1484-1492) / 59   Praecursor Siciliae.
(Forerunner of Sicily)
216 Alexander VI (1492-1503) /60   Bos Albanus in portu.
(Alban bull in the harbor)
217 Pius III (1503) /61   De parvo homine. (Of a small man)
218 Julius II (1503-1513) / 62   Fructus jovis juvabit. (Help
from the fruit of Jupiter)
219 Leo X (1513-1521) / 63   De craticula Politiana. (Of the
gridiron Poliziano)
220 Adrian VI (1522-1523) /64   Leo Florentius.
(Florentian, or Florens', Lion)
221 Clement VII (1523-1534) / 65   Flos pilaei aegri.
(Flower, or result, of the pills or medical balls)

222 Paul III (1534-1549) /66   Hiacynthus medicorum. (Physicians' hyacinthus)

Translations from this point forward date to 1797 or earlier. Therefore, the next part of this list contains no 20th- and 21st-century revisionist edits.

223 Julius III (1550-1555) / 67   De corona Montana. (The Mountain and Crown)

224 Marcellus II (1555) /68   Frumentum floccidum. (Bread-corn, suddenly perishing)

225 Paul IV (1555-1559) /69   De fide Petri. (Of the faith of Peter)

At this point, the prophecies become more significant. Many researchers believe that the original Malachy prophecies were written (or edited, based on Malachy's predictions) around the mid-1550s.

226 Pius IV (1559-1565) /70   Aesculapii pharmacum. (The medicine of the physician)

227 St. Pius V (1566-1572) /71   Angelus nemorosus. (Angel of the wood)

228 Gregory XIII (1572-1585) / 72   Medium corpus pilarum. (Middle body of balls)

229 Sixtus V (1585-1590) / 73   Axis in medietate signi. (Axle-tree is the midst of a sign)

230 Urban VII (1590) / 74   De rore caeli. (From heaven's dew)

231 Gregory XIV (1590-1591) / 75   De antiquitate Urbis. (From a city of antiquity)

232 Innocent IX (1591) / 76   Pia civitas in bello. (A city pious in war)

233 Clement VIII (1592-1605) / 77   Crux Romulea. (The Roman cross)

The first known publication of the Malachy prophecies were in 1595. So, everything from this point becomes very credible, regardless of the origins of the work.

234 Leo XI (1605) / 78   Undosus Vir. (A man gone as soon

as a wave)

235 Paul V (1605-1621) / 79   Gens perversa. (A perverse people)

236 Gregory XV (1621-1623) / 80   In tribulatione pacis. (In the work of peace)

237 Urban VIII (1623-1644) / 81   Lilium et rosa. (The lily and rose)

238 Innocent X (1644-1655) /82   Jucunditas crucis. (Joy of the cross)

239 Alexander VII (1655-1667) / 83   Montium custos. (Keeper of the mountains)

240 Clement IX (1667-1669) / 84   Sydus Olorum. (Constellation of swans)

241 Clement X (1670-1676) / 85   De flumine magno. (Of the great river)

242 Innocent XI (1676-1689) / 86   Bellua insatiabilis (An infallible beast)

243 Alexander VIII (1689-1691) / 87   Poenitentia gloriosa. (Glorious penitent)

244 Innocent XII (1691-1700) / 88   Rastrum in porta. (Rake in the gate)

245 Clement XI (1700-1721) / 89   Flores circumdati. (Flowers encompassing)

246 Innocent XIII (1721-1724) / 90   De bona Religione. (Of a good religion)

247 Benedict XIII (1724-1730) / 91   Miles in bello. (A soldier in war)

248 Clement XII (1730-1740) / 92   Columna excelsa. (A lofty pillar)

249 Benedict XIV (1740-1758) / 93   Animal rurale. (A rural animal)

250 Clement XIII (1758-1769) / 94   Rosa Umbriae. (Rose of Umbria)

251 Clement XIV (1769-1774) / 95   Ursus velox. (Quick sight)

252 Pius VI (1775-1799) / 96   Peregrinus Apostolicus. (Apostolic pilgrim)

253 Pius VII (1800-1823) / 97   Aquila rapax. (Ravenous eagle)

254 Leo XII (1823-1829) / 98   Canis et coluber. (Dog and snake)

255 Pius VIII (1829-1830) / 99   Vir religiosus. (Religious man)

256 Gregory XVI (1831-1846) / 100   De balneis hetruriae. (From the baths of Tuscany)

257 Pius IX (1846-1878) / 101   Crux de cruce. (Cross of cross)

258 Leo XIII (1878-1903) / 102   Lumen in caelo. (Light from heaven)

259 St. Pius X (1903-1914) / 103   Ignis ardent. (Flaming fire)

260 Benedict XV (1914-1922) / 104   Religio depopulata. (Religion laid waste)

261 Pius XI (1922-1939) / 105   Fides intrepida. (Faith fearless)

262 Pius XII (1939-1958) / 106   Pastor angelicus. (Angelic pastor)

263 John XXIII (1958-1963) / 107   Pastor et Nauta. (Both shepherd and sailor)

264 Paul VI (1963-1978) / 108   Flos florum. (Flower of flowers)

265 John Paul I (1978) / 109   De medietate Lunae. (Half of the Moon)

266 John Paul II (1978-2005) / 110   De labore Solis. (Labor of the Sun, or an eclipse)

267 Benedict XVI (2005-2013) / 111   Gloria olivae. (Glory of the olive)

268? /112...

In psecutione extrema S.R.E. sedebit.
Petrus Romanus, qui pascet oues in multis tribulationibus;
quibus transactis ciuitas septicollis diruetur, & Iudex tremêdus iudicabit populum suum.

Finis.

*With thanks to Mike Hebert and Zoltan of *Biblioteca Pleyades,* for preparing the basic numerical list, and providing it under a Creative Commons 3.0 Attribution license.

Prayers to Saint Michael

The following are the two prayers written by Pope Leo X, after hearing a conversation between Satan and Jesus.

Prayer to Saint Michael the Archangel

Most glorious Prince of the Heavenly Armies, Saint Michael the Archangel, defend us in "our battle against principalities and powers, against the rulers of this world of darkness, against the spirits of wickedness in high places" (Ephes., VI, 12).

Come to the assistance of men whom God has created to His likeness and whom He has redeemed at a great price from the tyranny of the devil. Holy Church venerates thee as her guardian and protector; to thee, the Lord has entrusted the souls of the redeemed to be led into heaven. Pray therefore the God of Peace to crush Satan beneath our feet, that he may no longer retain men captive and do injury to the Church. Offer our prayers to the Most High, that without delay they may draw His mercy down upon us; take hold of the dragon, "the old serpent, which is the devil and Satan," bind him and cast him into the bottomless pit "so that he may no longer seduce the nations" (Apoc. XX.2).

In the Name of Jesus Christ, our God and Lord, strengthened by the intercession of the Immaculate Virgin Mary, Mother of God, of Blessed Michael the Archangel, of the Blessed Apostles Peter and Paul and all the Saints, we confidently undertake to repulse the attacks and deceits of the devil. "Let God arise, let His enemies be scattered; let those who hate Him flee before Him. As smoke is driven away, so drive them away; as wax melts before the fire, so the wicked perish at the presence of God. " (Ps. 67)

V. Behold the Cross of the Lord, flee bands of enemies.

R. He has conquered, the Lion of the tribe of Juda, the offspring of David.

V. May Thy mercy, Lord, descend upon us.

R. As great as our hope in Thee. (at the "+" make the sign of the Cross)

We drive you from us, whoever you may be, every unclean spirit, all satanic powers, all infernal invaders, all wicked legions, assemblies and sects; in the Name and by the power of Our Lord Jesus Christ, + may you be snatched away and driven from the Church of God and from the souls made to the image and likeness of God and redeemed by the Precious Blood of the Divine Lamb. + Most cunning serpent, you shall no more dare to deceive the human race, persecute the Church, torment God's elect and sift them as wheat. + The Most High God commands you. + He with whom, in your great insolence, you still claim to be equal, "He who wants all men to be saved and to come to the knowledge of the truth" (1 Tim., 11.4). God the Father commands you. + God the Son commands you. + God the Holy Ghost commands you. + Christ, God's Word made flesh, commands you. + He who to save our race outdone through your envy, humbled Himself, becoming obedient even unto death" (Phil, 11,8); He who has built His Church on the firm rock and declared that the gates of hell shall not prevail against Her, because He will dwell with Her "all days even to the end of the world" (St. Mat., XXVIII,20). The sacred Sign of the Cross commands you, + as does also the power of the mysteries of the Christian Faith. + The glorious Mother of God, the Virgin Mary, commands you. + She who by her humility and from the first moment of her immaculate Conception, crushed your proud head. The faith of the Holy Apostles Peter and Paul and of the other Apostles commands you. + The blood of the Martyrs and the pious intercession of all the Saints command you. +

Thus, cursed dragon, and you, diabolical legions, we adjure you by the living God, + by the true God, + by the holy God, + by the God "who so loved the world that He gave up His only Son, that every soul believing in Him might not perish but have life everlasting" (St. John, III); stop deceiving human creatures and pouring out to them the poison of eternal damnation; stop harming the Church and hindering her liberty. Begone, Satan, inventor and master of all deceit, enemy of man's salvation. Give place to Christ in whom you have found none of your works; give place to the One, Holy, Catholic and Apostolic Church acquired by Christ at the price of His Blood. Stoop beneath the all-powerful Hand of God; tremble and flee when we invoke the Holy and terrible Name of Jesus, this Name which causes hell to tremble, this Name to which the Virtues, Powers and Dominations of Heaven are humbly submissive, this Name which the Cherubim and Seraphim praise unceasingly repeating: Holy, Holy, Holy is the Lord, the God of Armies.

V. O Lord, hear my prayer.

R. And let my cry come unto Thee.

V. May the Lord be with thee.

R. And with thy spirit.

Let us pray. God of Heaven, God of earth, God of Angels, God of Archangels, God of Patriarchs, God of Prophets, God of Apostles, God of Martyrs, God of Confessors, God of Virgins, God who has power to give life after death and rest after work, because there is no other God than Thee and there can be no other, for Thou art the Creator of all things, visible and invisible, of whose reign there shall be no end, we humbly prostrate ourselves before Thy glorious Majesty and we beseech Thee to deliver us by Thy power from all the tyranny of the infernal spirits, from their snares, their lies and their furious wickedness; deign, O Lord, to grant us Thy powerful protection and to keep us safe and sound. We beseech Thee through Jesus Christ Our Lord. Amen.

From the snares of the devil, deliver us, O Lord.

That Thy Church may serve Thee in peace and liberty, we beseech Thee to hear us.

That Thou may crush down all enemies of Thy Church, we beseech Thee to hear us.

(Holy water is sprinkled in the place where we may be.)

The Shorter Version (Originally said after Low Mass)

Saint Michael, the Archangel, defend us in battle; be our protection against the wickedness and snares of the devil.

May God rebuke him, we humbly pray, and do thou, O prince of the heavenly host, by the power of God, thrust into Hell, Satan and all the other evil spirits, who prowl throughout the world, seeking the ruin of souls. Amen.

Mother Shipton's Prophetic Poems

Mother Shipton, also known as Ursula Southeil (lived about 1488–1561) was born in Knaresborough, Yorkshire, England. She was known for her gift of prophecy. According to historian Samuel Pepys, even the *Royals* discussed her predictions after she foretold the Great Fire of London.

Some of her most noted poems weren't published until the late 1600s, but her accuracy and foresight have been acclaimed for centuries.

The following are two of her most famous poems, and may pertain to the last Pope and the world we live in today.

Mother Shipton's "future times" predictions

And now a word, in uncouth rhyme
Of what shall be in future time.

Then upside down the world shall be
And gold found at the root of tree
All England's sons that plough the land
Shall oft be seen with Book in hand
The poor shall now great wisdom know
Great houses stand in farflung vale
All covered o'er with snow and hail.

A carriage without horse will go
Disaster fill the world with woe.*
In London, Primrose Hill shall be
In centre hold a Bishop's See.

Around the world men's thoughts will fly
Quick as the twinkling of an eye.
And water shall great wonders do
How strange. And yet it shall come true.

Through towering hills proud men shall ride
No horse or ass move by his side.

Beneath the water, men shall walk
Shall ride, shall sleep, shall even talk.
And in the air men shall be seen
In white and black and even green.

A great man then, shall come and go
For prophecy declares it so.

In water, iron, then shall float
As easy as a wooden boat
Gold shall be seen in stream and stone
In land that is yet unknown.

And England shall admit a Jew
You think this strange, but it is true
The Jew that once was held in scorn
Shall of a Christian then be born.

A house of glass shall come to pass
In England. But Alas, alas
A war will follow with the work
Where dwells the Pagan and the Turk.

These states will lock in fiercest strife
And seek to take each others life.
When North shall thus divide the south
And Eagle build in Lions mouth
Then tax and blood and cruel war
Shall come to every humble door.

Three times shall lovely sunny France
Be led to play a bloody dance
Before the people shall be free
Three tyrant rulers shall she see.

Three rulers in succession be
Each springs from different dynasty.
Then when the fiercest strife is done
England and France shall be as one.

The British olive shall next then twine
In marriage with a german vine.
Men walk beneath and over streams
Fulfilled shall be their wondrous dreams.

For in those wondrous far off days
The women shall adopt a craze
To dress like men, and trousers wear
And to cut off their locks of hair
They'll ride astride with brazen brow
As witches do on broomstick now.

And roaring monsters with man atop
Does seem to eat the verdant crop
And men shall fly as birds do now
And give away the horse and plough.

There'll be a sign for all to see
Be sure that it will certain be.
Then love shall die and marriage cease
And nations wane as babes decrease.

And wives shall fondle cats and dogs
And men live much the same as hogs.

In nineteen hundred and twenty six
Build houses light of straw and sticks.
For then shall mighty wars be planned
And fire and sword shall sweep the land.

When pictures seem alive with movements free
When boats like fishes swim beneath the sea,
When men like birds shall scour the sky
Then half the world, deep drenched in blood shall die.

For those who live the century through
In fear and trembling this shall do.
Flee to the mountains and the dens
To bog and forest and wild fens.

For storms will rage and oceans roar
When Gabriel stands on sea and shore
And as he blows his wondrous horn
Old worlds die and new be born.

A fiery dragon will cross the sky
Six times before this earth shall die
Mankind will tremble and frightened be
for the sixth heralds in this prophecy.

For seven days and seven nights
Man will watch this awesome sight.
The tides will rise beyond their ken
To bite away the shores and then
The mountains will begin to roar
And earthquakes split the plain to shore.

And flooding waters, rushing in
Will flood the lands with such a din
That mankind cowers in muddy fen
And snarls about his fellow men.

He bares his teeth and fights and kills
And secrets food in secret hills
And ugly in his fear, he lies
To kill marauders, thieves and spies.

Man flees in terror from the floods
And kills, and rapes and lies in blood
And spilling blood by mankind's' hands
Will stain and bitter many lands.

And when the dragon's tail is gone,
Man forgets, and smiles, and carries on
To apply himself - too late, too late
For mankind has earned deserved fate.

His masked smile - his false grandeur,
Will serve the Gods their anger stir.
And they will send the Dragon back
To light the sky - his tail will crack
Upon the earth and rend the earth
And man shall flee, King, Lord, and serf.

But slowly they are routed out
To seek diminishing water spout
And men will die of thirst before
The oceans rise to mount the shore.

And lands will crack and rend anew
You think it strange. It will come true.

And in some far off distant land
Some men - oh such a tiny band
Will have to leave their solid mount

And span the earth, those few to count,
Who survives this [word not legible] and then
Begin the human race again.

But not on land already there
But on ocean beds, stark, dry and bare
Not every soul on Earth will die
As the Dragons tail goes sweeping by.

Not every land on earth will sink
But these will wallow in stench and stink
Of rotting bodies of beast and man
Of vegetation crisped on land.

But the land that rises from the sea
Will be dry and clean and soft and free
Of mankinds' dirt and therefore be
The source of man's new dynasty.

And those that live will ever fear
The dragons tail for many year
But time erases memory
You think it strange. But it will be.

And before the race is built anew
A silver serpent comes to view
And spew out men of like unknown
To mingle with the earth now grown
Cold from its heat and these men can
Enlighten the minds of future man.

To intermingle and show them how
To live and love and thus endow
The children with the second sight.
A natural thing so that they might
Grow graceful, humble and when they do
The Golden Age will start anew.

The dragon's tail is but a sign
For mankind's fall and man's decline.

And before this prophecy is done
I shall be burned at the stake, at one
My body singed and my soul set free

You think I utter blasphemy
You're wrong. These things have come to me
This prophecy will come to be.

*A second, *false* version of this poem -- notably altering
that stanza to claim the end of the world in 1881 -- was
published in 1862 by Charles Hindley. He was caught in
the fib. We're not sure he was embarrassed by it.

A second, prophetic poem by Mother Shipton

The signs will be there for all to read
When man shall do most heinous deed
Man will ruin kinder lives
By taking them as to their wives.

And murder foul and brutal deed
When man will only think of greed.
And man shall walk as if asleep
He does not look - he many not peep
And iron men the tail shall do
And iron cart and carriage too.

The kings shall false promise make
And talk just for talking's sake
And nations plan horrific war
The like as never seen before
And taxes rise and lively down
And nations wear perpetual frown.

Yet greater sign there be to see
As man nears latter century
Three sleeping mountains gather breath
And spew out mud, and ice and death.
And earthquakes swallow town and town,
In lands as yet to me unknown.

And christian one fights christian two
And nations sigh, yet nothing do
And yellow men great power gain
From mighty bear with whom they've lain.

These mighty tyrants will fail to do
They fail to split the world in two.
But from their acts a danger bred
An ague - leaving many dead.
And physics find no remedy
For this is worse than leprosy.

Oh many signs for all to see
The truth of this true prophecy.

More End Times Dates

Predicting the end of the world -- or at least the end of the world as we know it -- isn't new.

We found a reference to a 2800 BC prediction, described by Isaac Asimov in his *Book of Facts* (1979). Asimov said that an Assyrian clay tablet stated, "Our earth is degenerate in these latter days. There are signs that the world is speedily coming to an end. Bribery and corruption are common."

But, we're mindful of the mysteries of South and Central America, where sophisticated cultures seemed to disappear, leaving nothing but wonderful monuments in their wake. So, maybe some "worlds" *did* come to an end, long ago.

If you're looking for an exact date for the Rapture, Armageddon, the Apocalypse, or other End Time prediction, here are a few to choose among.

Any **Rosh Hashanah** -- the "head of the year" or the Feast of Trumpets -- is associated with the "last trumpet" that will signal the Rapture.

> 1 Corinthians, 15: 52 - *In a moment, in the twinkling of an eye, at the last trump: for the trumpet shall sound, and the dead shall be raised incorruptible, and we shall be changed.*

2013 - Recently discovered documents by Rasputin (1869 - 1916) reportedly say that the world will end on 23 August 2013 "when a fire shall devour all living things, then, the planet will be a quiet grave "

2016 - We haven't verified this date, but it's *said* that Pope Leo IX said, in either 1514 or 1516, "I will not see the end of the world, nor will you my brethren, for its time is long in the future, 500 years hence." There's a small problem with that report. Leo IX was Pope from 1049 - 1054. *Leo X* was Pope from 1513 - 1521. The 1514 *or* 1516 variation raises eyebrows. Sloppy handling of numbers like that makes us skeptical of related claims.

2017 - The Sword of God Brotherhood, described as a group of 25 believers in the south of France, believe that the end will come on 1 January 2017.

2023 - Theologist, author, and former BBC journalist Ian Gurney calculates that the final date "is less than 22 years away" from 2001. So, Judgment Day could be at any point up to and including 2023. (His book, *The Cassandra Prophecy,* reinterprets the Book of Daniel to provide a very different context than past theologians chose.)

2026 - The world's population was calculated to reach infinity at that year, according to the "doomsday equation," apparently based on $dy/dt = ky^{(1+c)}$ However, the initial calculations used figures from 1960. With the recent drop in birth rate, the input numbers probably move doomsday beyond 2026. If you're interested in this approach to end times, you'll need to learn more about the equation. It's not as simple as it looks.

2033 - Supposedly the 2000th anniversary of Christ's crucifixion, this date is problematic due to calendar changes since Bible times. However, our information may be incorrect on that point.

2037 - Popular 20th century psychic Jeane Dixon (1904 - 1997) predicted that Armageddon would take place in 2020, and the Second Coming of Christ would occur at some point between 2020 and 2037.

Not quite Biblical or the end times, we found this interesting bit of trivia. Or, it might be a hoax. Apparently, we'll be revisiting the Y2K panic on **January 19, 2038** when C programming languages will reset due to calendar or counting limitations. Rumor has it, they'll reset to 1 January 1970. We're not convinced that anyone will still be using the older C-related languages by 2038, but... only time will tell?

And, stepping outside the Christian context, a variety of religions and cultures have predicted end times. Among the most colorful and beloved are the Norse stories of Ragnarök or Ragnarøkkr.

A Google search for phrases such as "end times" or "apocalypse" will turn up hundreds of sites with far more end-of-the-world dates and theories.

As you can tell, we're skeptical of calendar-based predictions. They're fun, but we're more interested in the *larger* signs that point to a dramatic change. The reliability of Saint Malachy's predictions give us far more confidence, and -- to be honest -- a little more dread.

Urfa, Turkey - Safe Haven?

Did Jesus write or dictate a letter, during his lifetime? According to one apocryphal story, he did, and it promises safety to one community at the end times.

The letter -- generally discredited by Bible scholars -- was Jesus' reply to a letter from Abgarus Uchama, also known as Abgar V the Black or Abgarus V of Edessa.

Abgarus was ill and hoped to be healed. He'd also heard that some Jews were talking about injuring Jesus. So, he offered Jesus safe haven in his community.

Here is one of the most popular versions of Abgarus' letter to Jesus:

Abgarus Uchama to Jesus, the Good Physician Who has appeared in the country of Jerusalem, greeting:

> "I have heard of Thee, and of Thy healing; that Thou dost not use medicines or roots, but by Thy word openest (the eyes) of the blind, makest the lame to walk, cleansest the lepers, makest the deaf to hear; how by Thy word [also] Thou healest [sick] spirits and those who are tormented with lunatic demons, and how, again, Thou raisest the dead to life.

> And, learning the wonders that Thou doest, it was borne in upon me one of two things: either Thou hast come down from heaven, or else Thou art the Son of God, who bringest all these things to pass.

> Wherefore I write to Thee, and pray that thou wilt come to me, who adore Thee, and heal all the ill that I suffer, according to the faith I have in Thee.

> I also learn that the Jews murmur against Thee, and persecute Thee, that they seek to crucify Thee, and to destroy Thee. I possess but one small city, but it is beautiful, and large enough for us two to live in peace."

According to legend, Jesus wrote (or dictated to Hannan, a scribe or assistant) the following reply:

> 'Happy art thou who hast believed in Me, not having seen Me, for it is written of Me that those who shall see Me shall not believe in Me, and that those who shall not see Me shall believe in Me.
>
> As to that which thou hast written, that I should come to thee, (behold) all that for which I was sent here below is finished, and I ascend again to My Father who sent Me, and when I shall have ascended to Him I will send thee one of My disciples, who shall heal all thy sufferings, and shall give (thee) health again, and shall convert all who are with thee unto life eternal.
>
> And thy city shall be blessed forever, and the enemy shall never overcome it.'"

Assuming this story has at least a root in truth, which "enemy" did Jesus mean? Was it the adversary, or simply the usual "slings and arrows" of regional attacks?

Today, Abgarus' community is popularly known as Urfa. It's in the southern part of Turkey, about 35 miles north of the Syrian border.

It's a location to note, and see what happens there.

We think the Abgarus letter is probably fiction, but... well, as is often said, "Truth is stranger than fiction." So, we're not ready to dismiss the letter altogether.

The Last Pope? The Men to Watch

Several cardinals are extremely powerful but keep a low profile. If you were to mention *any* of their names — even to devout, never-miss-church-on-Sunday Catholics — the reply might be, "Umm... I *think* I know who he is..."

Cardinal Bertone

Some people are interested in the machinations of **Cardinal Tarcisio *Pietro* Evasio Bertone**, of *Romano* Cavanese. He was Pope Benedict XVI's Secretary of State, and also sat as leader of the Vatican, during the 13 days between Benedict XVI's departure and the election of Pope Francis.

We agree that he's made some astonishing mistakes, including the 2009 lifting of excommunication from four traditionalist bishops. It's not that the decision was necessarily wrong, but the handling of it in PR terms... it boggles the mind. If anything, he reminds us of the (literally) two-faced Professor Quirrell in the Harry Potter novels. When revealed as Voldemort's closest ally, Quirrell slipped back into his act and taunted, "...who would suspect p-p-poor, st-st-stuttering Professor Quirrell?"

Initially, we suspected that Bertone is a go-between, being manipulated by someone else or a small consortium.

However, he meets several criteria related to one translation of the Petrus Romanus prediction:

- His name includes Peter.
- He's a "Romanus" from Romano Cavanese.
- He sat as the leader of the Vatican, immediately *after* the departure of Pope Benedict XVI, the 111th Pope in St. Malachy's prediction.

In a recent interview with a German newspaper *Frankfurter Rundschau*, Cardinal Joachim Meisner put the spotlight on Bertone's problems. Meisner said that, in 2009 — speaking on behalf of several cardinals — he'd asked Pope Benedict XVI to dismiss Bertone, but the Pope refused.

At the moment, we're not sure if Cardinal Bertone may have served as Petrus Romanus. If he was, the next phase of the prophecy is in progress.

Cardinal Sodano

The next man to watch is **Cardinal Angelo Sodano**. He's the dean of the College of Cardinals, *the same job previously held by Pope Benedict XVI,* then-Cardinal Joseph Ratzinger.

Sodano is over 80 years old. In Vatican terms, that's not aged. He's still a force to be reckoned with.

Whether or not he influenced the conclave, Sodano *and those closest to him* should be studied closely. That includes micro-movements and news stories, even when Sodano and his associates *seem* to be playing low-profile roles.

We're not the first people to feel uneasy about Cardinal Sodano.

On 11 February 2013, in an op-ed article, *The Pope Could Still Right the Wrongs,* in the New York Times, Jason Berry mentioned "...Cardinal Angelo Sodano, the dean of the College of Cardinals and the man who, more than any other, embodies the misuse of power that has corrupted the church hierarchy."

It looks like Berry is right.

Sodano's history suggests a significant role in cover-ups related to sexual misconduct by members of the Catholic clergy. He's also found a path to power, while staying well out of the limelight.

An embarrassing moment in Chile was one of the first curious events that marks Sodano as a dark horse. Sodano became involved in a Chilean political issue. Though it put the Holy See at odds with the Chilean military government, Sodano arranged for four members of the MIR (Chile's *Revolutionary Left Movement*) to avoid charges and leave for Ecuador.

Then, in 1987 — possibly with Sodano's assistance — Pinochet contrived to have Pope John Paul II appear with him on the presidential balcony. It was a brilliant PR coup for Pinochet, and placed John Paul II in an uncomfortable political position. This was closely followed by a meeting that Sodano arranged with members of the opposition.

Seven Chilean priests ask Pope John Paul II to remove Cardinal Sodano.

How did the Pope respond?

He named Sodano the Holy See's *Secretary of the Council for the Public Affairs of the Church,* a post corresponding to that of a foreign minister. Then, on 1 December 1990, Pope John Paul II named Sodano to the highest post in the Roman Curia, that of *Secretary of State.*

It didn't stop there. Sodano became Cardinal-Priest of the titular church of *Santa Maria Nuova* on 28 June 1991.

During John Paul II's tenure at the Vatican, Sodano's name was linked to several failed attempts to bring wayward (and perhaps criminal) priests to justice.

But, despite the more advanced age of many cardinals, *Sodano is elderly.* He won't be around forever. (That's one reason to watch those he keeps close to him.) And, he's not the only powerful cardinal who gets his own way, sometimes overriding the efforts of his peers.

Cardinal Schönborn

Another figure to watch is **Cardinal Christoph Schönborn.** He was attributed as the leading (and, at the beginning of that conclave, perhaps the sole) force that guaranteed the election of Pope Benedict XVI.

We're not alone in that opinion. The National Catholic Reporter also described Schönborn as a "king-maker" during the 2005 conclave.

Cardinal Scola

In February 2012, when news broke that the Pope might be

assassinated, reports said that **Cardinal Angelo Scola** of Milan was being groomed as Benedict's replacement. We think that's a smokescreen, but we wouldn't rule him out as a player in this game.

After all, the real power — like the Wizard of Oz — might be the man hiding behind the curtain.

Cardinal Meisner

In an *odd* news report, **Cardinal Joachim Meisner** expressed justification for use of the "morning after" pill. On 31 January 2013, through his spokesman, Meisner said, "If, after a rape, a supplement is used with the intend of preventing fertilization, that is in my view justifiable."

A week later, the president of the World Federation of Catholic Medical Associations announced that Meisner's statement had been manipulated by the media, and then said that Meisner had been misinformed about the way the "morning after" pill works.

Those kinds of anomalies attract our attention. Generally, we're watching the men who avoid the headlines.
However, in moments of desperation, even the best covert operator can do something rash.

Cardinal Hummes and Cardinal Scherer

Cardinal Cláudio Hummes of Brazil is also on our radar. A lot of the evidence is quirky, like ley lines and odd events that connect both Hummes and Pope Francis. They also connect with **Cardinal Odilo *Pedro* Scherer**.
We're not ready to explain it in detail. We want something more substantial and... well, *reality*-based.

Nevertheless, we want to go on record as flagging them — especially Cardinal Hummes — among the figures that stand out in a broad field of potential *Petrus Romanus* players.

If you've been watching the coverage of Pope Francis, you've seen Cardinal Hummes. He's the man in red at the Pope's left elbow as Pope Francis spoke to the world. We're not ready to say that his expression was eerily like

Emperor Palpatine, but *something didn't look right.*

Keep an eye on him. He could be the nicest, kindest man in the world. We don't want to cast him in a bad light.

However... something seems *odd* there. We can't put our finger on it. With so much shifting in the church right now, we may not make sense of this for awhile.

We're already going out on a limb with many of our Petrus Romanus theories, so we decided to add these last two men — especially Hummes — to our list of interesting people.

Those cardinals — and their closest associates (whether obvious or entirely behind closed doors) — are the men we're watching right now. One or more of them might be *Petrus Romanus* or significant members of the end-game cast.

Like the Watergate investigative reporters, we recommend a "follow the money" approach to identify the most likely *Petrus* in Rome. After all, he's been crafty enough to stay hidden. We're not even sure he's among the cardinals.

Do not forget that Malachy's prophecy didn't say *Petrus Romanus* would be elected *Pope.* He's described as someone who holds leadership in the church. That's not the same thing as being Pope, and — since Malachy's description of *Petrus Romanus* doesn't follow the pattern of previous Papal clues, we're not certain he'll be an obvious player in this drama.

In the words of Doctor Who: *Don't blink.*

Bibliography

"Audience: God, Creation and free will." *The Vatican*
"Audience: God, Creation and free will." The Vatican
Today. N.p., 6 Feb. 2013. Web. 12 Feb. 2013.
<http://www.news.va/en/news/audience-god-creation-
and-free-will>.

Benedict, XVI. "Pope Benedict XVI announces his
resignation at end of month." *Vatican Radio*. N.p., 11 Feb.
2013. Web. 12 Feb. 2013.
<http://en.radiovaticana.va/articolo.asp?c=663815>.

Bzerbel. "New Pope Election Filled with the Number 13."
Planet Infowars. Infowarriors Worldwide, 13 Mar. 2013.
Web. 15 Mar. 2013.
<http://planet.infowars.com/uncategorized/new-pope-
election-filled-with-the-number-13>.

Chua-Eoan, Howard. "Pope of the Americas." Time World.
N.p., 13 Mar. 2013. Web. 15 Mar. 2013.
<http://world.time.com/2013/03/13/pope-of-the-
americas/>. "Cover Story: The September Pope." Time
Magazine. N.p., 9 Oct. 1978. Web. 15 Mar. 2013.

Chua-Eoan, Howard. "The Resignation of Pope Benedict
XVI: Is It Health? Or Politics? Or Both?" *Time Magazine*.
N.p., 11 Feb. 2013. Web. 12 Feb. 2013.
<http://world.time.com/2013/02/11/the-resignation-of-
pope-benedict-xvi-is-it-health-or-politics-or-both/>.

Cross, Donna Woolfolk. "Pope Joan." *Morgana's*
Observatory. N.p., n.d. Web. 14 Feb. 2013.
<http://www.dreamscape.com/morgana/popejoan.htm>.

Crystal, Ellie. "Mother Shipton's Prophecies."
CrystalLinks. Ellie Crystal, n.d. Web. 12 Feb. 2013.
<http://www.crystalinks.com/mother_shipton.html>.

Cutler, David. "Timeline: Benedict steps down as Pope."
Ed. Will Waterman. *Reuters*. N.p., n.d. Web. 12 Feb. 2013.
<http://www.reuters.com/article/2013/02/11/us-pope-

resigns-benedict-idUSBRE91A0IP20130211>.

"European Prophets – 1b." *Biblioteca Pleyades*. N.p., n.d.
Web. 12 Feb. 2013.
<http://www.bibliotecapleyades.net/profecias/esp_profec
ia01c1b.htm>.

Evans, Becky. "Bless him, he's had a makeover: Francis
ditches his glasses as he goes to church on first morning as
Pope." Daily Mail Online. N.p., 14 Mar. 2013. Web. 15 Mar.
2013. <http://www.dailymail.co.uk/news/article-
2293150/Pope-Francis-I-ditches-glasses-goes-church-
morning-Pope.html>.

Feather, White. "The Ninth and Last Sign About to Come
True?" *WHITE FEATHER SPEAKS ABOUT THE NINE
SIGNS*. Hawkeye Engineering, n.d. Web. 20 Feb. 2013.
<http://www.twohawks.com/hopi/hopififthworld.shtml>.

Grattan-Flood, William. "St. Malachy." The Catholic
Encyclopedia. Vol. 9. New York: Robert Appleton
Company, 1910. 13 Feb. 2013
<http://www.newadvent.org/cathen/09565a.htm>.

Hogue, John. *The Last Pope – Revisited*. N.p.: n.p., 2006.
Print.

Jamieson, Alastair, and Ian Johnston. "Pope Francis:
Argentina's Cardinal Jorge Mario Bergoglio is new Catholic
leader." NBC News. N.p., 14 Mar. 2013. Web. 15 Mar. 2013.
<http://worldnews.nbcnews.com/_news/2013/03/13/172
90508-pope-francis-argentinas-cardinal-jorge-mario-
bergoglio-is-new-catholic-leader?lite>.

"Jan Hus." *Wikipedia*. N.p., 11 Feb. 2013. Web. 12 Feb.
2013. <http://en.wikipedia.org/wiki/Jan_Hus>.

Korston, Gerald. "Paging 'Peter the Roman': Debunking
the Prophecy of St. Malachy." Catholic Online. N.p., 10
Mar. 2013. Web. 15 Mar. 2013.
<http://www.catholic.org/comments/news/50051/?
page=1>.

"The last time a pope resigned: 1415." *Momaha*. N.p., 11
Feb. 2013. Web. 12 Feb. 2013.

<http://www.omaha.com/article/20130211/MOMS16/302
119865/1685>.

Lawlor, H. J. *St. Bernard of Clairvaux's Life of St.
Malachy of Armagh*. London: Macmillan, 1920. Print.

"The List of Popes." The Catholic Encyclopedia. Vol. 12.
New York: Robert Appleton Company, 1911. 13 Feb. 2013
<http://www.newadvent.org/cathen/12272b.htm>.

Marrs, Texe. "The Pope, the Devil, and the Masonic
Lodge." *Jesus is Savior*. N.p., n.d. Web. 12 Feb. 2013.
<http://www.jesus-is-savior.com/False
%20Religions/Roman%20Catholicism/pope-devil-
masonic_lodge.htm>.

Martin, Ernest. "Ancient Cities of Seven Hills and Bible
Prophecy." *THE Bible   Study website*. N.p., n.d. Web. 19
Feb. 2013. <http://www.biblestudy.org/
prophecy/ancient-cities-of-seven-hills-and-bible-
prophecy.html>.

"Papal Prophecies – End Days." *His Sheep*. Art & Sue Renz,
n.d. Web. 12 Feb. 2013.
<http://www.hissheep.org/catholic/papal_prophecies.htm
l>.

"Pope convokes consistory for canonization of three
Blessed." *The Vatican Today*. N.p., 4 Feb. 2013. Web. 12
Feb. 2013. <http://www.news.va/en/news/pope-
convokes-consistory-for-canonization-of-three>.

"The Prophecy of St. Malachy." *Follow This*. N.p., n.d.
Web. 13 Feb. 2013. <http://www.followthissite.com/st-
malachy.php>.

"Prophecy of the Popes." *Wikipedia*. N.p., 13 Feb. 2013.
Web. 13 Feb. 2013.
<http://en.wikipedia.org/wiki/Prophecy_of_the_Popes>.

"Prophesies of the Antichrist By Early Church Fathers."
Unity Publishing. N.p.,   n.d. Web. 20 Feb. 2013.
<http://www.unitypublishing.com/prophecy/
AntichristbySaints.htm>.

"Prophétie de Jean de Vatiguerro." *Barbieux – Poupart*.

N.p., n.d. Web. 12 Feb. 2013.
<http://www.barbieux.org/static/ovni/prophetes/vatiguer
.php>.

"Ring of the Fisherman." Wikipedia. N.p., 14 Mar. 2013.
Web. 15 Mar. 2013.
<http://en.wikipedia.org/wiki/Ring_of_the_Fisherman>.

"Saint Malachy." *Wikipedia*. N.p., 12 Feb. 2013. Web. 13
Feb. 2013.
<http://en.wikipedia.org/wiki/Saint_Malachy>.

Santos, Fabio. "Jean de Vatiguerro." *Blog MidiaeProfecia*.
N.p., 8 Feb. 2013. Web. 12 Feb. 2013.
<http://midiaeprofecia.blogspot.com/2013/02/jean-de-
vatiguerro.html>.

Urban, Sylvanus. *The Gentleman's Magazine and
Historical Chronicle*. Vol. 67. London: John Nichols, 1797.
Print.

Walsh, Michael. "Benedict XVI resignation: The two-pope
problem." BBC News. N.p., 26 Feb. 2013. Web. 15 Mar.
2013. <http://www.bbc.co.uk/news/
world-europe-21616503>.

Ware, James. *The Whole Works Concerning Ireland,
Revised and Improved*. Vol. 3. Dublin: A. Reilly, 1746.
Print.

Zoltan, and Mike Hebert. "List of Popes with References to
St. Malachy's Prophecies." *Biblioteca Pleyades*. N.p., n.d.
Web. 13 Feb. 2013.
<http://www.bibliotecapleyades.net/vatican/esp_vatican1
4g.htm>.

About the authors

Dace Allen (DaceAllen.com) specializes in "lost" history, especially related to the Pleiades and similar influences on Earth's history.

Dace is the author of *The Pleiadians Files: Hidden and Ancient Records* and -- as of early 2013 -- is still working on a sequel to that best-selling study. In the meantime, Dace keeps getting sidetracked by studies like the Saint Malachy predictions.

Sarah Skye majored in Art History at Harvard University and promptly turned her interests to New Age topics. (Well, there's not a lot you can do with a degree in Art History. There's teaching and working in museums, but neither of those appealed to her... something she didn't consider when she chose her major.) Now she's a freelance writer. She's penned over 1000 articles for websites including Suite 101 and Bella Online, as well as a variety of magazines. She's also completed some work as a ghostwriter. This was her first book under her own name.

She's also the author of the March 2013 book, *North Korea - What's Behind the Headlines.*

Dace and Sarah have also written a more focused, condensed book about the Petrus Romanus topic: *Petrus Romanus - Who, Where, When.* It contains similar information, but not so much trivia, and it's organized a little differently. If you know someone who's interested in this topic, the shorter book might be a good introduction.

Did you like this book? Hate it? Wish we'd included more of something... or less?

Tell your friends about this book, and be sure to leave your thoughts in a review at Amazon.com.

We *do* read our reviews, and we can improve future books if we know your honest opinions of our work.

Made in United States
North Haven, CT
29 October 2023